D1078169

EUGENE O'NEILL

Born in New York City in 1888, son of a well-known actor, Eugene O'Neill spent a year at Princeton University (1906) before signing on as a seaman and travelling widely. Following a period in a sanatorium recovering from TB, he wrote his first play, *A Wife for a Life*. In 1916 he joined the Provincetown Players, who produced the first of his plays to be staged, *Bound East for Cardiff*, as well as other early work. His Broadway debut came in 1920 with *Beyond the Horizon*, which also won him a Pulitzer Prize.

The next fourteen years saw the premieres of some twenty new plays, including *The Emperor Jones* (1920), *Anna Christie* (1921), which won a second Pulitzer Prize, *The Hairy Ape* (1922), *All God's Chillun Got Wings* (1924), *Desire Under the Elms* (1924), *The Great God Brown* (1926), *Strange Interlude* (1928), which won another Pulitzer, *Mourning Becomes Electra* (1931), a trilogy reworking the *Oresteia*, *Ah! Wilderness* (1933) and *Days Without End* (1933), after which thirteen years elapsed with no new play reaching the stage, though he continued writing. Two more plays were produced during his lifetime: *The Iceman Cometh* in 1946, though written in 1939, and *A Moon for the Misbegotten* in 1947, though it only reached Broadway ten years later, after his death in 1953.

Plays staged posthumously include *Long Day's Journey into Night* (1956), which won a fourth Pulitzer, *A Touch of the Poet* (1958) and *More Stately Mansions* (1962). He was three times married, his third wife, Carlotta Monterey, surviving him. In 1936 he became the first American dramatist to win the Nobel Prize for Literature.

EUGENE O'NEILL
THE HAIRY APE
&
ALL GOD'S CHILLUN GOT WINGS

Introduction by
Christine Dymkowski

ROYAL NATIONAL THEATRE
London

NICK HERN BOOKS

The Hairy Ape & All God's Chillun Got Wings first published in this edition in 1993 jointly by the Royal National Theatre, London, and Nick Hern Books Limited, 14 Larden Road, London W3 7ST

Reprinted in 1995

The Hairy Ape first published in Great Britain by Jonathan Cape in 1923
All God's Chillun Got Wings first published by Jonathan Cape in 1925;
Cover photograph of Eugene O'Neill by courtesy of the Raymond Mander & Joe Mitcheson Theatre Collection

Set in Baskerville by Edna A Moore, ✺ Tek Art, Addiscombe, Surrey
Printed and bound in India by Seagull Books, Calcutta.

British Library Cataloguing in Publication Data: a catalogue record for this book is available from the British Library

ISBN 1 85459 151 7

Contents

Biographical Sketch of Eugene O'Neill (1888–1953)

'Some day James O'Neill will best be known as the father of
Eugene O'Neill': so Eugene himself frequently boasted
throughout 1912. The claim struck those who heard it not with a
sense of the young man's prescience but of his presumption.
Nothing in his life so far had given any indication that in less
than a decade he would be a playwright to reckon with, shaking
up the American theatre and shaping a new American drama.
Instead, he seemed more likely to become one of the pipe-
dreamers who eternally inhabit Harry Hope's no-chance saloon in
his own *The Iceman Cometh*.

Born on 16 October 1888, to the respected and accomplished
actor James O'Neill and his wife Ella Quinlan O'Neill, Eugene
was to find his family an overwhelming force in his life and to
make it the almost constant subject of his plays. He was the
O'Neills' third son: the eldest, Jamie, had been born ten years
before; a second son, Edmund, had followed five years later. Life
was not easy for the O'Neills and their two young children; James
was already touring the country in *Monte Cristo*, the vehicle that
would spell both his financial success and his artistic defeat (he
succumbed to popular demand and played the role 4000 times
between 1883 and 1912). Ella, convent-educated and proper,
loved her husband but felt she had married beneath her; she
never took to James's theatrical life or to his theatrical friends.
However, the couple could not bear to be parted, and Ella, with
great reluctance, frequently left the children in the care of her
mother to join her husband on the road. Early in 1885, on one of
these occasions, Jamie contracted measles and disobeyed
instructions to stay away from his brother; Edmund became ill
and died.

Such family history might in another case seem irrelevant, but
it is crucial for an understanding of Eugene O'Neill and of his
work. Ella did not want any more children after Edmund's death,
but James, convinced that it would help solace her, persuaded
her to have another. The result was a family tragedy that
blighted all four lives, and not least the new baby, Eugene. In an
attempt to counteract the pain of an exceedingly difficult birth,
Ella was unwittingly precipitated into the morphine addiction

from which she would suffer for the next twenty-six years. James, Jamie, and Eugene were greatly affected by Ella's distraction and withdrawal from reality, but Jamie and Eugene endured a private hell of guilt: Jamie for inadvertently killing the brother whose loss had had such drastic consequences, and Eugene for having been born at all.

Fifteen when he learned of his mother's addiction, Eugene no longer had to fear the mental illness he had up till then suspected he would inherit; the truth, however, was worse. Although summers were spent at the family's home in New London, Connecticut, their haphazard existence in a succession of hotels while James was on tour had already given Eugene a sense of rootlessness that plagued him all his life. Now, guilty that his birth had effected such misery, he developed a deep sense of unbelonging that at times manifested itself as a death-wish. He rejected his parents' Catholicism and, under Jamie's influence, began to drink and to visit brothels. Both Jamie and Eugene, displacing their anger, blamed their father for their mother's condition, accusing him of hiring a 'quack' to attend Ella at Eugene's birth. In fact, even reputable doctors at that time prescribed morphine, and in doses so low that addiction was by no means inevitable.

Eugene entered Princeton in 1906, but only stayed a year, having spent most of his time drinking, cutting classes, and following his own reading interests. It was at this time that he discovered Nietzsche's *Thus Spake Zarathustra*, which together with the works of Strindberg, became his personal bible. After leaving Princeton, he worked for a short time in a New York office job arranged by his father. In the city's Greenwich Village, Hell's Kitchen, and Tenderloin districts, he began to frequent the dives he would immortalise in many of his plays and also began to write poetry. O'Neill remained a heavy drinker for years, though he never drank while writing; in 1926 he gave up alcohol completely, lapsing only a few times thereafter.

Wishing to escape from a romantic entanglement with Kathleen Jenkins, O'Neill let his father arrange for him to join a mining expedition in Honduras in October 1909. Nevertheless, because Kathleen was pregnant, he agreed to marry her shortly before his departure. Having contracted malaria after a few months in Central America, Eugene returned to the US and, without visiting his wife and new-born son (Eugene O'Neill, Jr.), joined his father's company on tour, checking tickets. Shortly afterwards, in June 1910, O'Neill boarded the *Charles Racine*, a Norwegian windjammer, as a working passenger on its two-month voyage to

Buenos Aires. O'Neill loved the sea – he was throughout his life a keen and able swimmer – and now had the chance to experience a sailing life first-hand; it was an experience he would exploit in many of his early plays.

O'Neill remained in Argentina for several months, occasionally working but mainly living as a down-and-out; he sailed back to New York in March 1911 on the S.S. *Ikala*, this time as a member of the crew. He stayed in New York long enough to arrange for a divorce, living in an alcoholic haze at a downtown bar and flophouse called Jimmy-the-Priest's. In July, he signed onto the S.S. *New York* as an ordinary seaman for its voyage to Southampton; he returned in August on the S.S. *Philadelphia* as an able-bodied seaman, a qualification of which he was to remain proud for the rest of his life. Resuming his destitute way of life at Jimmy-the-Priest's – though he regularly attended the performances of Dublin's Abbey Players, who were visiting New York – O'Neill sank progressively into a depression that in January 1912 culminated in a suicide attempt. When he had sufficiently recovered, he rejoined his father's company for a few months, this time taking on small acting roles.

1912 seemed to mark a watershed in O'Neill's life, as evidenced both by his boasting of future fame and by his setting of many of his most autobiographical plays in that year. Moving to New London, Connecticut, in the summer, he worked as a reporter for the *Telegraph*, continued to write poetry, and developed a mild case of tuberculosis. By the end of the year, he was at the Gaylord Farm Sanatorium, where he was to remain for six months. During that time he decided to become a playwright.

Returning to New London in summer 1913 and boarding with the Rippins, a local family, he began to write one-act plays based on his own experiences. O'Neill's father subsidised their publication as *Thirst and Other One Act Plays* in August 1914, and the following September O'Neill enrolled in Professor George Pierce Baker's famous play-writing course at Harvard. Although he did not particularly distinguish himself in the class, his disdain for easy formulaic success made clear his ambition to be an original dramatist.

After his year at Harvard, O'Neill returned to New York and became somewhat involved in the political and intellectual life of Greenwich Village, frequenting the Golden Swan saloon, familiarly known as the 'Hell Hole'. He submitted some plays to the adventurous Washington Square Players, who had recently formed in reaction to the glib, commercial offerings of Broadway; however, the Players were not so adventurous as to stage any of O'Neill's works.

His first real theatrical opportunity came in June 1916 when he accompanied his friend Terry Carlin to Provincetown, at the tip of Massachusetts's Cape Cod. Then, as now, Provincetown boasted a flourishing artists' colony each summer. The previous year, the writer Susan Glaspell, her husband Jig Cook, and other vacationing Greenwich Village friends had staged an impromptu production, marking the birth of what would become the Provincetown Players. When O'Neill arrived in Provincetown, the group were desperately short of plays for their new season. O'Neill offered them *Bound East for Cardiff*, which premiered on 28 July 1916, the first-ever performance of an O'Neill play. His work with the Players also led to his involvement in Greenwich Village's radical circle, which included John Reed, Louise Bryant, Mabel Dodge, and Floyd Dell, among others.

The Provincetown Players' success was such that in September 1916 they moved operations to Greenwich Village, acquiring a base on Macdougal Street, which at O'Neill's suggestion was named the Playwrights' Theatre. During the group's eight subscription seasons between 1916 and 1922, O'Neill had ample opportunity to experiment without regard to commercial considerations. For example, *The Emperor Jones*, staged by the Provincetown Players in November 1920, not only had an African-American for its protagonist but was also considerably shorter than standard length. Despite its unconventionality, the play marked the group's first popular success: following its scheduled performances at the Playwrights' Theatre, it moved uptown to Broadway for an unlimited run. When the original Provincetown Players disbanded, O'Neill, together with the designer Robert Edmond Jones and the critic-producer Kenneth Macgowan, founded the Experimental Theatre, Inc., in 1923. The triumvirate ran the Playwrights' Theatre, now renamed the Provincetown Playhouse, from 1923–25 and the Greenwich Village Theatre from 1924–26.

The Provincetown Players' success with *The Emperor Jones* was not O'Neill's first theatrical triumph. *Beyond the Horizon*, which opened at the Morosco Theatre on Broadway in February 1920, was greeted by extremely favourable reviews, transferred for an extended run, and brought O'Neill his first Pulitzer Prize (the second drama award in the prize's four-year history). This success was quickly followed by another: *Anna Christie* opened in November 1921 and brought him a second Pulitzer. He was to win the award twice more, for *Strange Interlude* in 1928 and posthumously in 1956 for *Long Day's Journey into Night*, a record that has not been matched.

By the time of his early success, O'Neill's personal life had undergone considerable change: married for a second time, to the writer Agnes Boulton, he had become a father again with the birth of Shane Rudraighe O Neill on 30 October 1919 (his last child, Oona, who later married Charlie Chaplin, was born on 14 May 1925). His father had died in August 1920, having lived long enough to see his younger son succeed; in the year prior to his death, Eugene had finally recognised his father's long-standing forbearance and support and had become friendly with him. Ironically, O'Neill's own neediness so dominated his life that he could never be a father to his own children, who all suffered the neglect for which O'Neill had bitterly and unfairly resented his own father. Eugene Jr. committed suicide at the age of forty, and Shane was for many years a heroin addict.

Within three years of his father's death, O'Neill was the sole survivor of his original family: his mother died of a brain tumour in February 1922, and Jamie had drunk himself to death by November 1923. Their deaths freed O'Neill to explore the dark side of his family life, which he proceeded to do in plays as diverse (and variously successful) as *All God's Chillun Got Wings*, *Dynamo*, *Long Day's Journey into Night*, and *A Moon for the Misbegotten*. Further change was in store: in 1927 O'Neill left Agnes Boulton for Carlotta Monterey, who became his third wife in July 1929. Misogynist, desirous of a mother, unable to separate love from hate, O'Neill had difficult relationships with women. He found his own guilt at his desertion of Agnes too difficult to deal with, and, as he later did with his children, manufactured grievances against her. His third marriage fulfilled his desire that his wife should be completely dedicated to his own interests, but it was a stormy one with cruelty on both sides.

O'Neill was quintessentially an autobiographical playwright: many of his protagonists are recognisable O'Neill figures, sharing the playwright's own lean build and dark deep-set eyes. All of his experiences found their way onto the stage, from the sea-going life depicted in early one-act plays like *Bound East for Cardiff* to his ambivalence about parenthood in *The First Man* to his Strindbergian view of marital relations in *Welded*. This need to depict, explain, and justify himself had considerable ramifications for his role as a playwright: he could not really regard theatre as the collaborative activity it so patently is. Time and again. O'Neill lamented the process of staging his plays, complaining that the ideal play he had seen in his head never existed in production. Whereas playwrights generally welcome the new life that actors and directors bring to their work, O'Neill saw it as a betrayal. So strongly did he feel this that he virtually never went to any productions of his plays, only attending rehearsals in order to advise and to cut when necessary.

In addition, his personal investment in what he wrote often blinded him to its deficiencies: he could be convinced that inferior works like *Welded*, *Dynamo*, and *Days Without End* were undervalued and misjudged. For example, while *Dynamo* ostensibly focused on the relationship between humankind, machines, and religion, it was really O'Neill's working out of his ambivalent relationship to his mother: small wonder that it made more sense to O'Neill than to the critics. However, at his best, O'Neill was able to transmute his personal experiences into the most powerful of dramas, as he does in works like *Long Day's Journey into Night* and *The Iceman Cometh*.

Although he wrote essentially to please himself and to exorcise his private demons (as early as 1924 he claimed that 'Writing is my vacation from living'), O'Neill was genuinely interested in stretching American drama beyond the narrow confines it had so far inhabited. His experiments were many: trying to make the audience share a character's hallucination in *Where the Cross is Made*, extending the audience's endurance by writing four- and five-hour long plays, using set location schematically in *Beyond the Horizon*, incorporating expressionistic elements in *The Hairy Ape*, masking the characters in *The Great God Brown*, modernising the use of the aside in *Strange Interlude*, developing a modern equivalent for the Greek sense of tragedy in *Desire Under the Elms* and *Mourning Becomes Electra*, creating an ambitious play-cycle detailing a critical history of America through the story of one family in *A Tale of Possessors Self-Dispossessed* (of which only *A Touch of the Poet* was completed to his satisfaction).

Although his achievements won him the Nobel Prize for literature in 1936, in the last years of his life O'Neill was something of a has-been. He had suffered for years from a hand tremor, caused by a rare degenerative disease of the cerebellum that attacks the motor system, which made writing increasingly difficult; by 1943, it had become impossible. Since O'Neill had never been able to compose at a typewriter or by dictation, his writing career, apart from some revisions, was effectively over. Furthermore, he was extremely depressed by the Second World War: it made his writing seem of little consequence and the staging of his work even less important and appropriate. Consequently, he refused to authorise productions of new plays; none appeared between *Days Without End* in 1933 and *The Iceman*

Cometh in 1946. When the latter was finally staged, the inadequate production did little to restore interest in O'Neill's work.

Throughout his life, O'Neill had roamed far in search of a home and a sense of belonging: New York, Connecticut, Provincetown, Bermuda, France, Georgia, California. Sometime before his death on 27 November 1953, O'Neill struggled up from his bed to complain 'I knew it, I knew it! Born in a goddam hotel room and dying in a hotel room!' Only with the posthumous revival of *The Iceman Cometh* and the first production of *Long Day's Journey into Night* in 1956 did his reputation, like his life, come full circle.

Christine Dymkowski
Lecturer in Drama and Theatre Studies
Royal Holloway and Bedford New College
University of London

Introduction to the Plays

O'Neill wrote *The Hairy Ape* at white heat in two and a half weeks
in December 1921, though it had had a long genesis. In 1917, he
had written a short story, also called 'The Hairy Ape', about his
friend Driscoll, a stoker on the S.S. *Philadelphia*, who also figures
in the *Glencairn* plays and the story 'Tomorrow'. Driscoll, who
seemed to O'Neill the embodiment of raw strength and vitality,
had inexplicably committed suicide in 1915 by jumping
overboard during a transatlantic crossing. O'Neill later explained
that the 'germ idea' for *The Hairy Ape* derived from his 'search for
an explanation of why Driscoll, proud of his animal superiority
and in complete harmony with his limited conception of the
universe, should kill himself' (quoted in Gelb, p. 488). The
answer finally yielded by this search – that Yank, the Driscoll
character, had lost his sense of 'belonging' – had its roots in
O'Neill's own deepest experience of never having belonged.

In depicting Mildred Douglas, the society woman whose disgust
shakes Yank's belief in himself, O'Neill drew on his own time
aboard the *Philadelphia* and *New York*: he had felt patronized by
passengers going about their business while he scrubbed the
decks. But *The Hairy Ape*, in its use of expressionistic elements to
depict Yank's experience, also shows external forces at work on
the playwright. Although O'Neill always claimed that the only
influence on *Ape* was his own earlier play, *The Emperor Jones*,
Sheaffer relates that before writing it O'Neill had seen and
admired the German Expressionist film *The Cabinet of Dr Caligari*
and had also read Georg Kaiser's Expressionist play *From Morn to
Midnight*, the plot of which resembles O'Neill's (*Son & Artist*,
p. 76). An even more important influence was Susan Glaspell's
play, *The Verge*, which O'Neill had read by August 1921. Linda
Ben-Zvi has persuasively demonstrated the similarities in
structure, setting, and expressionistic detail between the two
plays; indeed, the '*murderous hug*' with which O'Neill's gorilla
dispatches the 'hairy ape' Yank mirrors the Glaspell heroine's
strangling embrace of her near-soulmate Tom. Sheaffer also
points out that the autobiographical *Education of Henry Adams*
helped shape the mystical attitude to machines that Yank evinces,
while Carl Sandburg's poem 'Smoke and Steel' contributed to his

celebration of steel (*Son & Artist*, pp. 73, 307).

The Hairy Ape opened at the Playwrights' Theatre, New York, on 9 March 1922; a Provincetown Players production, it was directed by James Light with assistance from Arthur Hopkins. The part of Yank was played by Louis Wolheim, an actor of burly physique and tremendous force; he was one of only three actors ever to satisfy O'Neill in his realization of a character. Although the sets, designed by Robert Edmond Jones and Cleon Throckmorton, were abstract, Wolheim played the part with an intense emotional realism, the ferocity of which sometimes frightened Mary Blair, who played Mildred. A couple of years later, O'Neill explained in an interview with the New York *Herald Tribune* (16 March 1924) why such a performance was essential to his play and why he disavowed any connection with German Expressionism:

> I personally do not believe that an idea can be readily put over to an audience except through characters. When it sees 'A Man' and 'A Woman' – just abstractions, it loses the human contact by which it identifies itself with the protagonist of the play. . . . But the character Yank remains a man and everyone recognizes him as such. (quoted in Cargill, p. 111).

Nevertheless, in a letter to Robert Sisk some years later, O'Neill explained that his method blended expressionism and naturalism: '"Yank" is a living recognizable human being but he is also a symbol in a sort of modern Morality Play' (15 March 1935, quoted in *Selected Letters*, p. 445).

The Hairy Ape was the first O'Neill play to use masks symbolically; their success in the production encouraged the playwright's subsequent experiments with them in plays as diverse as *All God's Chillun Got Wings*, *The Great God Brown*, *Lazarus Laughed*, and *Days Without End*. On this occasion, however, the idea came from designer Blanche Hays as a way of fulfilling O'Neill's desire for uniformity in the Scene 5 society chorus: O'Neill wanted the actors to look alike and to be dressed alike, '*A procession of gaudy marionettes . . . with something of the relentless horror of Frankensteins in their detached, mechanical unawareness*'. Wainscott describes their thin, cheesecloth masks as 'expressionless, ominous face masks, just slightly larger than life size' and apparently 'fitted to the actors' hats, which [were] lodged tightly in place to allow the actors' jerky movements' (*Staging O'Neill*, p. 117). O'Neill later wished that he had used masks more extensively in the play; he felt that from the beginning of the fourth scene, all the characters should be masked, 'even the familiar faces of [Yank's] mates in the forecastle', to reflect Yank's experience ('Second

Thoughts', reprinted in Cargill, p. 119).

Besides using stylized movement and abstract sets, the production also effectively employed expressionistic sound: for example, one critic wrote that 'the loud laughter of [Yank's] mates [in Scene 4] suddenly [became] rhythmic, like the fearful tattoo of a drum' (quoted in Wainscott, p. 114). Even the gorilla of the final scene, which could easily have proved an embarrassment, was highly successful, at least in critic Stark Young's opinion. He noted that the ape emerged 'so fearfully out of the cage. It was fine, extraordinary, out of class with any animal motive [sic] I have ever known on the stage' (quoted in Wainscott, p. 121). The actor's costume consisted of a papier-mâché head mask and a suit fashioned from dyed goat skins.

Although reviews were mixed, the production of *The Hairy Ape* was a popular success, eventually transferring to the Plymouth Theater on Broadway and enjoying a long run of 127 performances. Hopkins, who sponsored the transfer, insisted that Mary Blair was not glamorous enough for an uptown audience and replaced her with Carlotta Monterey, who many years later was to become O'Neill's third wife. Although O'Neill regretted Blair's forced departure from the cast, his experience of *The Hairy Ape*'s production was unusually happy, 'one of [my] most satisfying times in the theatre' (from O'Neill's 16 May 1944 letter to Theresa Helburn, quoted in *Selected Letters*, p. 558). The play, together with *The Great God Brown*, was to remain one of O'Neill's life-long favourites.

The Hairy Ape was the last new O'Neill play to be staged by the Provincetown Players; *All God's Chillun Got Wings* was the first new O'Neill play to be staged by Experimental Theatre, Inc., at the Provincetown Playhouse, formerly the Playwrights' Theatre. The timing of the plays marked not only a professional but also a personal transition for O'Neill: *The Hairy Ape* had opened on the same night that the body of his mother Ella O'Neill arrived in New York for burial, and, while O'Neill was writing *All God's Chillun* between September and December 1923, his brother Jamie died. The consequent freedom felt by O'Neill to explore his family experience is immediately evident in the play.

The title of *Chillun* is taken from an African-American spiritual: 'I got wings/You got wings/All God's chillun' got wings' (quoted in Gelb, p. 536). The fraught marriage between Jim Harris, who is black, and Ella Downey, who is white, has some of its origins in external fact and fiction. The Gelbs point out similarities to Strindberg's *The Dance of Death* with its love-hate relationship between the sexes (*O'Neill*, pp. 233–34); Sheaffer recounts the heavily publicized suicide of Etta Johnson, white wife of the black heavyweight boxing champion, while O'Neill was a reporter in New London, Connecticut, in 1912 (*Son & Artist*, p. 119). O'Neill's 1922 Work Diary refers to it as the 'Play of Johnny T. – negro who married white woman – base play on his experience *as I have seen it intimately* – but no reproduction, see it only as man's' (quoted in Floyd, pp. 53, 176).

As his biographers acknowledge, however, O'Neill's experience of his own parents' relationship was a much greater influence on the play; its significance is marked by his bestowing their names on the two central characters. Ella Downey's isolation, her sense of superiority to and dependence on her husband, and her mental imbalance all reflect Ella O'Neill's own history, while the racial prejudice that Jim Downey suffers parallels the anti-Irish bigotry experienced by James O'Neill. Furthermore, as Sheaffer points out, the transposition of the O'Neills' relationship to an inter-racial milieu may have been inspired by James O'Neill's own fondness for quoting Othello's lines justifying his marriage to Desdemona (*Son & Playwright*, p. 58; *Son & Artist*, p. 118).

Chillun, directed by James Light and designed by Cleon Throckmorton, opened on 15 May 1924 amidst great pre-production controversy. Paul Robeson had been cast as Jim opposite Mary Blair as Ella at a time when such a part would normally have been played by a blacked-up white actor; general public outrage followed when word leaked out that the script called for Blair to kiss Robeson's hand. City officials, having no authority to forbid performances in a non-public theatre, tried to stop it by withholding permission for child actors to appear in Scene 1; however, the simple expedient of the director's reading the scene to the audience allowed the performance to proceed.

O'Neill continued his experiments with expressionism in *Chillun*, though the production was not able to fulfil the Act 2 stage directions that the Harris parlour should appear shrunken in Scene 2 and still more so in Scene 3. Consequently, the African tribal mask lost most of the power that O'Neill had envisaged for it: by Scene 2 it was to '*look unnaturally large and domineering*'. Percy Hammond commented in his review that its influence was less obvious on stage than it had been in the text: 'Though this symbol of jungle ancestry was spot-lighted more or less subtly, and though Miss Blair cursed it very well indeed, it lacked the hypnotic allure that it has in the printed version', (New York *Herald Tribune*, 16 May 1924, p. 10). However, Hammond was also immune to other, more successfully expressionistic devices in the play, complaining of the lack of 'illusion' in many scenes; for example, Jim and Ella 'emerged theatrically from the church [in Act 1, Scene 4] wherein they were married and [[Jim] stood spectacularly upon the top step, like Oedipus, while theatrical groups of black and whites gathered on each side of him'. O'Neill later wished that he had masked 'all save the seven leading characters' of the play, since 'the secondary figures are part and parcel of the [play's] Expressionistic background' ('Second Thoughts', reprinted in Cargill, p. 119).

Hammond's review is fairly typical of critical response, which was generally unenthusiastic about the play. However, the public flocked to see it, encouraged by the controversy it had engendered. Sheaffer relates that *Chillun* alternated in repertory for a while with a revival of *The Emperor Jones*, then played on its own for a month, and after a summer break played to non-subscription audiences for another two months at the Greenwich Village Theatre (*Son & Artist*, p. 144). Despite its disappointing reviews, *Chillun* achieved a total run of about 105 performances.

All God's Chillun was revived frequently in London throughout the twenties and thirties, with productions at the Gate Theatre Salon in 1926, the Gate Theatre Studio in 1928, and the Court Theatre in 1929. Paul Robeson appeared in the play opposite Flora Robson at the Embassy Theatre in 1933; the production, which opened on 13 March, transferred to the Piccadilly Theatre on 3 April and played for nearly four more weeks. The play was also revived by the left-wing Unity Theatre in February 1946; programme notes stress an agitprop approach to the play. However, while *Chillun* was progressive when first written, it now appears both dated and retrograde; modern sensibilities are more likely to be embarrassed and offended rather than moved by Jim's declaration to Ella at the close of Act 1, Scene 3. Sinking to his knees and in '*a frenzy of self-abnegation*', Jim '*beats his head on the flagstones*' as he promises to 'give my life and my blood and all the strength that's in me to give you peace and joy to become – your slave! . . . – your black slave that adores you as sacred!'

The Hairy Ape also received contemporaneous London productions. First seen at The Gate Theatre in January 1928, it was subsequently revived on 11 May 1931 at the Ambassadors Theatre; directed by James Light, the production starred a much-praised Paul Robeson as Yank. Unlike *Chillun*, however, the play has recently enjoyed two impressive revivals. The first was a visually stunning production by Berlin's Schaubühne Company; directed by Peter Stein and designed by Lucio Fanti, the play was performed in German as part of the World Theatre Season at the National's Lyttelton Theatre from 11–16 May 1987. Much of the play's power was lost, however, even to German-speakers, by the long intervals necessitated by massive and complicated scenery.

English-speaking audiences had a better chance to judge the

play in the Bolton Octagon production of 8–30 March 1991.
Directed by Andrew Hay and designed by Mick Bearwash, the
production featured a 'cold, hard set of steel scaffolding' (Robin
Thornber, *Guardian*, 12 March 1991) that allowed an 'intelligent
and often spectacular' use of 'physical heights' (Jo Say,
Manchester *Uptown*, 12 March 1991). Thornber commented that
the production 'turn[ed] the text into a sort of musical theme
that's just one element in an intensely visual, physical theatrical
experience' whose 'images hit home hard'. Cliff Howells's
critically-praised performance as Yank seems to have achieved the
precise blend of naturalism and expressionism that O'Neill
wished for the play: Thornber felt 'compel[led] to share [Yank's]
outraged dignity' but saw him as 'everyone who has been belittled
by life'; Michael Schmidt, finding the character 'entirely
unattractive', focused 'not on a single man's tragedy but on the
tragedy of class division and the dehumanisation of modern
industry' (*Daily Telegraph*, 13 March 1991). Such responses
suggest that, in the modern theatre at least, O'Neill's Hairy Ape
still 'belongs'.

Christine Dymkowski
April 1992

Sources

Ben-Zvi, Linda. 'Susan Glaspell and Eugene O'Neill', *The Eugene O'Neill
    Newsletter* (Boston), Vol. 6, No. 2 (Summer/Fall 1982), pp. 21–29.
—————————. 'Susan Glaspell and Eugene O'Neill: The Imagery of
    Gender', *The Eugene O'Neill Newsletter* (Boston), Vol. 10, No. 1 (Spring
    1986), pp. 22–27.
Bogard, Travis and Jackson R. Breyer, eds. *Selected Letters of Eugene
    O'Neill.* New Haven and London: Yale University Press, 1988.
Cargill, Oscar, et ai., eds. *O'Neill and His Plays: Four Decades of Criticism.*
    New York: New York University Press, 1961.
Floyd, Virginia, ed. *Eugene O'Neill at Work: Newly Released Ideas for Plays.*
    New York: Frederick Ungar, 1981.
Gelb, Arthur and Barbara. *O'Neill.* New York: Harper, 1960.
Miller, Jordan Y. *Eugène O'Neill and the American Critic: A Summary and
    Bibliographical Checklist.* Second edition, revised. Hamden, Connecticut:
    Archon, 1973.
Ranald, Margaret Loftus. *The Eugene O'Neill Companion.* Westport, Conn.,
    & London: Greenwood, 1984.

Sheaffer, Louis. *O'Neill: Son & Playwright*. London: Dent, 1968.
——————. *O'Neill: Son & Artist*. London: Paul Elek, 1973.
Wainscott, Ronald H. *Staging O'Neill: The Experimental Years, 1920–1934*. New Haven and London: Yale University Press, 1988.

I would also like to thank Sue Cusworth of RHBNC for help both in tracing British productions of O'Neill's plays and in obtaining copies of reviews and programmes.

List of O'Neill's Produced Plays

Title	Year Written*	First Production	First London Production
The Web	1913–14	39th Street Theatre, New York 17 March 1924	
Thirst	1913–14	Wharf Theatre, Provincetown, Mass. Summer 1916	
Fog	1913–14	Playwrights' Theater, New York 5 January 1917	
Bound East for Cardiff	1913–14	Wharf Theatre, Provincetown, Mass. 28 July 1916	(see S.S. Glencairn)
Servitude	1913–14	Skylark Theatre N.Y. International Airport 22 April 1960	
Abortion	1913–14	Key Theatre, New York 27 October 1959	
The Movie Man	1914	Key Theatre, New York 27 October 1959	

Play	Year		
The Sniper	1915	Playwright's Theater, New York 16 February 1917	Gate Theatre 30 August 1926
Before Breakfast	1916	Playwrights' Theater, New York 1 December 1916	Everyman Theatre 17 April 1922
Ile	1916–17	Playwrights' Theater, New York 30 November 1917	Everyman Theatre 15 June 1921
In the Zone	1916–17	Comedy Theater, New York (Washington Square Players) 31 October 1917	Everyman Theatre 12 June 1925
The Long Voyage Home	1916–17	Playwrights' Theater, New York 2 November 1917	(see *S.S. Glencairn*)
The Moon of The Caribbees	1916–17	Playwrights' Theater, New York 20 December 1918	
S.S. Glencairn (*Bound East for Cardiff, In the Zone, Moon of the Caribbees,* and *Long Voyage Home*)		Barnstormer's Barn Provincetown, Massachusetts 14 August 1924	Mercury Theatre 9 June 1947

Title	Year Written*	First Production	First London Production
The Rope	1918	Playwrights' Theater, New York 26 April 1918	
The Dreamy Kid	1918	Playwrights' Theater, New York 31 October 1919	(Festival Theatre, Cambridge 14 May 1928)
Beyond the Horizon	1918	Morosco Theater, New York 3 February 1920	Regent Theatre (The Repertory Players) 31 January 1926
Where the Cross is Made	1918	Playwrights' Theater, New York 22 November 1918	Arts Theatre 27 October 1927
The Straw	1918–19	Greenwich Village Theater, New York 10 November 1921 (after an out-of-town try-out)	
Exorcism	1919	Playwrights' Theater, New York 26 March 1920	
Chris (1st version of Anna Christie)	1919	Apollo Theater, Atlantic City, N.J. 8 March 1920	
Gold	1920	Frazee Theater, New York 1 June 1921	

Anna Christie	1920	Vanderbilt Theater, New York 2 November 1921	Strand Theatre 10 April 1923
The Emperor Jones	1920	Playwrights' Theater, New York 1 November 1920	Ambassadors' Theatre 10 September 1925
Diff'rent	1920	Playwrights' Theater, New York 27 December 1920	Everyman Theatre 4 October 1921
The First Man	1921	Neighborhood Playhouse, New York 4 March 1922	
The Hairy Ape	1921	Playwrights' Theater, New York 9 March 1922	Gate Theatre 26 January 1928
The Fountain	1921–22	Greenwich Village Theater, New York 10 December 1925	
Welded	1922–23	39th Street Theater, New York 17 March 1924	The Playroom Six 16 February 1928
All God's Chillun Got Wings	1923	Provincetown Playhouse, New York 15 May 1924	Gate Theatre 8 November 1926

Title	Year Written*	First Production	First London Production
The Ancient Mariner (adaptation)	1924	Provincetown Playhouse (previously Playwrights' Theater), New York 6 April 1924	
Desire Under The Elms	1924	Greenwich Village Theater, New York 11 November 1924	Gate Theatre 24 February 1931
Marco Millions	1923–25	Guild Theater, New York 9 January 1928	Westminster Theatre 26 December 1938 (also produced at Festival Theatre, Cambridge, 1932)
The Great God Brown	1925	Greenwich Village Theater, New York 23 January 1926	Strand Theatre (Stage Society) 19 June 1927
Lazarus Laughed	1925–26	Pasadena Community Playhouse, California 9 April 1928	
Strange Interlude	1926–27	John Golden Theater, New York 30 January 1928	Lyric Theatre 3 February 1931
Dynamo	1928	Martin Beck Theater, New York 11 February 1929	
Mourning Becomes Electra	1929–31	Guild Theater, New York 26 October 1931	Westminster Theatre 19 November 1937

Ah! Wilderness	1932	Nixon Theater, Pittsburgh, Pennsylvania 25 September 1933 (out-of-town tryout before New York opening at Guild Theater, 2 October 1933)	Westminster Theatre 4 May 1936
Days Without End	1932–33	Plymouth Theater, Boston, Mass. 27 December 1933 (out-of-town tryout before New York opening at Guild Theater, 8 January 1934)	Grafton Theatre (Stage Society) 3 February 1935
A Touch of the Poet	1935–42	Royal Dramatic Theatre, Stockholm, Sweden 29 March 1957 (first American production at Helen Hayes Theater, New York, 2 October 1958)	Young Vic Theatre 20 January 1988 (also produced at Ashcroft Theatre, Croydon, 16 September 1963)
More Stately Mansions	1936–42	Royal Dramatic Theatre, Stockholm, Sweden 11 September 1962 (first American production at Ahmanson Theater, Los Angeles, California, 12 November 1967)	Greenwich Theatre 19 September 1974

Title	Year Written*	First Production	First London Production
The Iceman Cometh	1939	Martin Beck Theater, New York 9 October 1946	Arts Theatre 29 January 1958
Long Day's Journey into Night	1939–41	Royal Dramatic Theatre, Stockholm, Sweden 10 February 1956 (first American production at Helen Hayes Theater, New York, 7 November 1956)	Globe Theatre 24 September 1958 (transfer from Lyceum Theatre, Edinburgh, 8 September 1958)
Hughie	1941–42	Royal Dramatic Theatre, Stockholm, Sweden 18 September 1958	Duchess Theatre 18 June 1963
A Moon for the Misbegotten	1943	Hartman Theater, Columbus, Ohio (Guild Theater production) 20 February 1947	Arts Theatre 20 January 1960

*Dates of composition are approximate.

THE HAIRY APE

A Comedy of Ancient and Modern Life

Characters

ROBERT SMITH 'YANK'
PADDY
LONG
MILDRED DOUGLAS
HER AUNT
SECOND ENGINEER
A GUARD
A SECRETARY OF AN ORGANIZATION
STOKERS, LADIES, GENTLEMEN, etc.

Scenes

Scene One
The fireman's forecastle of an ocean liner. An hour after sailing
from New York.

Scene Two
Section of promenade deck, two days out. Morning.

Scene Three
The stokehole. A few minutes later.

Scene Four
Same as Scene One. Half an hour later.

Scene Five
Fifth Avenue, New York. Three weeks later.

Scene Six
An island near the city. The next night.

Scene Seven
In the city. About a month later.

Scene Eight
In the city. Twilight of the next day.

Time
The modern.

Scene One

Scene. The firemen's forecastle of a transatlantic liner an hour after sailing from New York for the voyage across. Tiers of narrow, steel bunks, three deep, on all sides. An entrance in rear. Benches on the floor before the bunks. The room is crowded with men, shouting, cursing, laughing, singing – a confused, inchoate uproar swelling into a sort of unity, a meaning – the bewildered, furious, baffled defiance of a beast in a cage. Nearly all the men are drunk. Many bottles are passed from hand to hand. All are dressed in dungaree trousers and heavy ugly shoes. Some wear vests, but the majority are stripped to the waist.

The treatment of this scene, or of any other scene in the play, should by no means be naturalistic. The effect sought is a cramped space in the bowels of a ship, imprisoned by white steel. The lines of bunks, the uprights supporting them, cross each other like the steel framework of a cage. The ceiling crushes down upon the men's heads. They cannot stand upright. This accentuates the natural stooping posture which shovelling coal and the resultant over-development of back and shoulder muscles have given them. The men themselves should resemble those pictures in which the appearance of Neanderthal Man is guessed at. All are hairy-chested, with long arms of tremendous power, and low, receding brows above their small, fierce, resentful eyes. All the civilized white races are represented, but except for the slight differentiation in colour of hair, skin, eyes, all these men are alike.

The Curtain rises on a tumult of sound. YANK is seated in the foreground. He seems broader, fiercer, more truculent, more powerful, more sure of himself than the rest. They respect his superior strength – the grudging respect of fear. Then, too, he represents to them a self-expression, the very last word in what they are, their most highly developed individual.

VOICES.
   Gif me trink dere, you!
   'Ave a wet!
   Salute!
   Gesundheit!
   Skoal!
   Drunk as a lord, God stiffen you!
   Here's how!

Luck!
Pass back that bottle, damn you!
Pourin' it down his neck!
Ho, Froggy! Where the devil have you been?
La Touraine.
I hit him smash in yaw, py Gott!
Jenkins – the First – he's a rotten swine –
And the coppers nabbed him – and I run --
I like peer better. It don't pig head gif you.
A slut, I'm sayin'! She robbed me aslape –
To hell with 'em all!
You're a bloody liar!
Say dot again! (*Commotion. Two men about to fight are pulled apart.*)
No scrappin' now!
Tonight –
See who's the best man!
Bloody Dutchman!
Tonight on the for'ard square.
I'll bet on Dutchy.
He packa da wallop, I tella you!
Shut up, Wop!
No fightin' maties. We're all chums, ain't we?

(*A voice starts bawling a song.*)

> 'Beer, beer, glorious beer!
> Fill yourselves right up to here.'

YANK (*for the first time seeming to take notice of the uproar about him, turns around threateningly – in a tone of contemptuous authority*). Choke off dat noise! Where d'yuh get dat beer stuff? Beer, hell! Beer's for goils – and Dutchmen. Me for somep'n wit a kick to it! Gimme a drink, one of youse guys. (*Several bottles are eagerly offered. He takes a tremendous gulp at one of them; then, keeping the bottle in his hand, glares belligerently at the owner, who hastens to acquiesce in this robbery by saying:*) All right-o, Yank. Keep it and have another. (YANK *contemptuously turns his back on the crowd again. For a second there is an embarrassed silence. Then –*)

VOICES.
We must be passing the Hook.
She's beginning to roll to it.
Six days in hell – and then Southampton.
Py Yesus, I vish somepody take my first vatch for me!

Gittin' seasick, Square-head?
Drink up and forget it!
What's in your bottle?
Gin.
Dot's nigger trink.
Absinthe? It's doped. You'll go off your chump, Froggy!
Cochon!
Whisky, that's the ticket!
Where's Paddy?
Going asleep.
Sing us that whisky song, Paddy.

They all turn to an old, wizened Irishman who is dozing, very drunk, on the benches forward. His face is extremely monkey-like with all the sad, patient pathos of that animal in his small eyes.

Singa da song, Caruso Pat!
He's gettin' old. The drink is too much for him.
He's too drunk.

PADDY (*blinking about him, starts to his feet resentfully, swaying, holding on to the edge of a bunk*). I'm never too drunk to sing. 'Tis only when I'm dead to the world I'd be wishful to sing at all. (*With a sort of sad contempt.*) 'Whisky, Johnny,' ye want? A chanty, ye want? Now that's a queer wish from the ugly like of you, God help you. But no matther. (*He starts to sing in a thin, nasal, doleful tone:*)

Oh, whisky is the life of man!
Whisky! O Johnny! (*They all join in on this.*)
Oh, whisky is the life of man!
Whisky for my Johnny! (*Again chorus.*)
Oh, whisky drove my old man mad!
Whisky! O Johnny!
Oh, whisky drove my old man mad!
Whisky for my Johnny!

YANK (*again turning around scornfully*). Aw hell! Nix on dat old sailing-ship stuff! All dat bull's dead, see? And you're dead, too, yuh damed old Harp, on'y yuh don't know it. Take it easy, see. Give us a rest. Nix on de loud noise. (*With a cynical grin.*) Can't youse see I'm tryin' to tink?

ALL (*repeating the word after him as one with the same cynical amused mockery*). Think! (*The chorused word has a brazen, metallic quality, as if their throats were phonograph horns. It is followed by a general uproar of hard, barking laughter.*)

VOICES.
> Don't be cracking your head wid ut, Yank.
> You gat headache, py yingo!
> One thing about it – it rhymes with drink!
> Ha, ha, ha!
> Drink, don't think!
> Drink, don't think!
> Drink, don't think!

> (*A whole chorus of voices has taken up this refrain, stamping on the floor, pounding on the benches with fists.*)

YANK (*taking gulp from his bottle – good-naturedly*). Aw right. Can de noise. I got yuh de foist time. (*The uproar subsides. A very drunken sentimental tenor begins to sing:*)

> Far away in Canada,
> Far across the sea,
> There's a lass who fondly waits
> Making a home for me –

YANK (*fiercely contemptuous*). Shut up, yuh lousey boob! Where d'yuh get dat tripe? Home? Home, hell! I'll make a home for yuh! I'll knock yuh dead. Home! T'hell wit home! Where d'yuh get dat tripe? Dis is home, see? What d'yuh want wit home? (*Proudly.*) I runned away from mine when I was a kid. On'y too glad to beat it, dat was me. Home was lickings for me, dat's all. But yuh can bet your shoit no one ain't never licked me since! Wanter try it, any of youse? Huh! I guess not. (*In a more placated but still contemptuous tone.*) Goils waitin' for yuh, huh? Aw, hell! Dat's all tripe. Dey don't wait for no one. Dey'd double-cross yuh for a nickel. Dey're all tarts, get me? Treat 'em rough, dat's me. To hell wit 'em. Tarts, dat's what, de whole bunch of 'em.

LONG (*very drunk, jumps on a bench excitedly, gesticulating with a bottle in his hand*). Listen 'ere, Comrades! Yank 'ere is right. 'E says this 'ere stinkin' ship is our 'ome. And 'e says as 'ome is 'ell. And 'e's right! This is 'ell. We lives in 'ell, Comrades – and right enough we'll die in it. (*Raging.*) And who's ter blame, I arsks yer? We ain't. We wasn't born this rotten way. All men is born free and ekal. That's in the bleedin' Bible, maties. But what d'they care for the Bible – them lazy, bloated swine what travels first cabin? Them's the ones. They dragged us down till we're on'y wage slaves in the bowels of a bloody ship, sweatin', burnin' up, eatin' coal-dust! Hit's them's ter blame – the damned capitalist clarss! (*There had been a gradual murmur of*

*contemptuous resentment rising among the men until now he is
interrupted by a storm of catcalls, hisses, boos, hard laughter.*)

VOICES.
   Turn it off!
   Shut up!
   Sit down!
   Closa da face!
   Tamn fool! (*Etc.*)

YANK (*standing up and glaring at* LONG). Sit down before I
   knock yuh down! (LONG *makes haste to efface himself.* YANK *goes
   on contemptuously.*) De Bible huh? De Cap'tlist class, huh? Aw nix
   on dat Salvation Army-Socialist bull. Git a soap-box! Hire a
   hall! Come and be saved, huh? Jerk us to Jesus, huh? Aw
   g'wan! I've listened to lots of guys like you, see. Yuh're all
   wrong. Wanter know what I tink? Yuh ain't no good for no
   one. Yuh're de bunk. Yuh ain't got no noive, get me? Yuh're
   yellow, dat's what. Yellow, dat's you. Say! What's dem slobs in
   de foist cabin got to do wit us? We're better men dan dey are,
   ain't we? Sure! One of us guys could clean up de whole mob
   wit one mit. Put one of 'em down here for one watch in de
   stokehole, what'd happen? Dey'd carry him off on a stretcher.
   Dem boids don't amount to nothin'. Dey're just baggage. Who
   makes dis old tub run? Ain't it us guys? Well den, we belong,
   don't we? We belong and dey don't. Dat's all. (*A loud chorus of
   approval.* YANK *goes on.*) As for dis bein' hell – aw, nuts! Yuh
   lost your noive, dat's what. Dis is a man's job, get me? It
   belongs. It runs dis tub. No stiffs need apply. But yuh're a stiff,
   see? Yuh're yellow, dat's you.

VOICES (*with a great hard pride in them*).
   Right-o!
   A man's job!
   Talk is cheap, Long.
   He never could hold up his end.
   Divil take him!
   Yank's right. We make it go.
   Py Gott, Yank say right ting!
   We don't need no one cryin' over us.
   Makin' speeches.
   Throw him out!
   Yellow!
   Chuck him overboard!
   I'll break his jaw for him!

They crowd around LONG *threateningly.*

YANK (*half good-natured again – contemptuously*). Aw, take it easy. Leave him alone. He ain't woith a punch. Drink up. Here's how, whoever owns dis. (*He takes a long swallow from his bottle. All drink with him. In a flash all is hilarious amiability again, back-slapping, loud talk, etc.*)

PADDY (*who has been sitting in a blinking, melancholy daze – suddenly cries out in a voice full of old sorrow*). We belong to this, you're saying? We make the ship to go, you're saying? Yerra then, that Almighty God have pity on us! (*His voice runs into the wail of a keen, he rocks back and forth on his bench. The men stare at him, startled and impressed in spite of themselves.*) Oh, to be back in the fine days of my youth, ochone! Oh, there was fine beautiful ships them days – clippers wid tall masts touching the sky – fine strong men in them – men that was sons of the sea as if 'twas the mother that bore them. Oh, the clean skins of them, and the clear eyes, the straight backs and full chests of them! Brave men they was, and bold men surely! We'd be sailing out, bound down round the Horn maybe. We'd be making sail in the dawn, with a fair breeze, singing a chanty song wid no care to it. And astern the land would be sinking low and dying out, but we'd give it no heed but a laugh, and never a look behind. For the day that was, was enough, for we was free men – and I'm thinking 'tis only slaves do be giving heed to the day that's gone or the day to come – until they're old like me. (*With a sort of religious exaltation.*) Oh, to be scudding south again wid the power of the Trade Wind driving her on steady through the nights and the days! Full sail on her! Nights and days! Nights when the foam of the wake would be flaming wid fire, when the sky'd be blazing and winking wid stars. Or the full of the moon maybe. Then you'd see her driving through the grey night, her sails stretching aloft all silver and white, not a sound on the deck, the lot of us dreaming dreams, till you'd believe 'twas no real ship at all you was on but a ghost ship like the Flying Dutchman they say does be roaming the seas for evermore widout touching a port. And there was the days, too. A warm sun on the clean decks. Sun warming the blood of you, and wind over the miles of shiny green ocean like strong drinks to your lungs. Work – aye, hard work – but who'd mind that at all? Sure, you worked under the sky, and 'twas work wid skill and daring to it. And wid the day done, in the dog-watch, smoking me pipe at ease, the look out would be raising land maybe, and we'd see the mountains of South Americy wid the red fire of the setting sun painting their white tops and the clouds floating by them! (*His tone of exaltation ceases. He goes on mournfully.*) Yerra, what's the use of talking? 'Tis a dead man's whisper. (*To* YANK *resentfully.*) 'Twas them days men belonged to ships, not now. 'Twas them days a ship was part of the sea, and a man was part of a ship, and the sea joined all together and made it one. (*Scornfully.*) Is it one wid this you'd be, Yank -- black smoke from the funnels smudging the sea, smudging the decks -- the bloody engines pounding and throbbing and shaking -- wid divil a sight of sun or a breath of clean air -- choking our lungs wid coal-dust -- breaking our backs and hearts in the hell of the stokehole -- feeding the bloody furnace -- feeding our lives along wid the coal, I'm thinking -- caged in by steel from a sight of the sky like bloody apes in the Zoo! (*With a harsh laugh.*) Ho-ho, divil mend you! Is it to belong to that you're wishing? Is it a flesh and blood wheel of the engines you'd be?

YANK (*who has been listening with a contemptuous sneer, barks out the answer*). Sure ting! Dat's me! What about it?

PADDY (*as if to himself -- with great sorrow*). Me time is past due. That a great wave wid sun in the heart of it may sweep me over the side sometime I'd be dreaming of the days that's gone!

YANK. Aw, yuh crazy Mick! (*He springs to his feet and advances on* PADDY *threateningly -- then stops, fighting some queer struggle within himself -- lets his hands fall to his sides -- contemptuously.*) Aw, take it easy. Yuh're aw right at dat. Yuh're bugs, dat's all -- nutty as a cuckoo. All dat tripe yuh been pullin' -- Aw, dat's all right. On'y it's dead, get me? Yuh don't belong no more, see. Yuh don't get de stuff. Yuh're too old. (*Disgustedly.*) But aw say, come up for air once in a while, can't yuh? See what's happened since yuh croaked. (*He suddenly bursts forth vehemently, growing more and more excited.*) Say! Sure! Sure I meant it! What de hell -- Say, lemme talk! Hey! Hey, you old Harp! Hey, youse guys! Say, listen to me -- wait a moment -- I gotter talk, see. I belong and he don't. He's dead but I'm livin'. Listen to me! Sure I'm part of de engines! Why de hell not! Dey move, don't dey? Dey're speed, ain't day? Dey smash trou, don't dey? Twenty-five knots a' hour! Dat's goin' some! Dat's new stuff! Dat belongs! But him, he's too old. He gets dizzy. Say, listen. All dat crazy tripe about nights and days; all dat crazy tripe about stars and moons; all dat crazy tripe about suns and winds, fresh air and de rest of it -- aw hell, dat's all a dope dream! Hittin' de pipe of de past, dat's what he's doin'. He's old and don't belong no more. But me, I'm young! I'm in de pink! I move wit it! It, gets me! I mean de ting dat's de guts of all dis. It ploughs trou all de tripe he's been sayin'. It blows dat up! It knocks dat dead! It slams dat offen de face of de oith! It, get me! De engines and de coal and de smoke and all de rest of it! He can't breathe and swallow coal-dust, but I kin, see? Dat's fresh air for me! Dat's food for me! I'm new, get me? Hell in de stokehole? Sure! It takes a man to work in hell. Hell, sure, dat's my fav'rite climate. I eat it up! I git fat on it! It's me makes it hot! It's me makes it roar! It's me make it move! Sure, on'y for me everyting stops. It all goes dead, get me? De noise and smoke and all de engines movin' de woild, dey stop. Dere ain't nothin' no more! Dat's what I'm sayin'. Everyting else dat makes de woild move, somep'n makes it move. It can't move witout somep'n else, see? Den yuh get down to me. I'm at de bottom, get me! Dere ain't nothin' foither. I'm de end! I'm de start! I start somep'n and de woild moves! It – dat's me! – de new dat's moiderin' de old! I'm de ting in coal dat makes it boin; I'm steam and oil for de engines; I'm de ting in noise dat makes yuh hear it; I'm smoke and express trains and steamers and factory whistles; I'm de ting in gold dat makes it money! And I'm what makes iron into steel! Steel, dat stands for de whole ting! And I'm steel – steel – steel! I'm de muscles in steel, de punch behind it! (*As he says this he pounds with his fist against the steel bunks. All the men, roused to a pitch of frenzied self-glorification by his speech, do likewise. There is a deafening metallic roar, through which* YANK'*s voice can be heard bellowing.*) Slaves, hell! We run de whole woiks. All de rich guys dat t'ink dey're somep'n, dey ain't nothin'! Dey don't belong. But us guys, we're in de move, we're at de bottom, de whole ting is us! (PADDY *from the start of* YANK'*s speech has been taking one gulp after another from his bottle, at first frightenedly, as if he were afraid to listen, then desperately, as if to drown his senses, but finally has achieved complete indifferent, even amused, drunkenness.* YANK *sees his lips moving. He quells the uproar with a shout.*) Hey, youse guys, take it easy! Wait a moment! De nutty Harp is sayin' somep'n.

PADDY (*is heard now – throws his head back with a mocking burst of laughter*). Ho-ho-ho-ho-ho –

YANK (*drawing back his fist, with a snarl*). Aw! Look out who yuh're givin' the bark!

PADDY (*begins to sing the 'Miller of Dee' with enormous good-nature*):

 'I care for nobody, no, not I,
 And nobody cares for me.'

YANK (*good-natured himself in a flash, interrupts* PADDY *with a slap*

on the bare back like a report). Dat's de stuff! Now yuh're gettin'
wise to somep'n. Care for nobody, dat's de dope! To hell wit
'em all! And nix on nobody else carin'. I kin care for myself,
get me! (*Eight bells sound, muffled, vibrating through the steel walls
as if some enormous brazen gong were embedded in the heart of the
ship. All the men jump up mechanically, file through the door silently
close upon each other's heels in what is very like a prisoners' lockstep.
YANK slaps PADDY on the back.*) Our watch, yuh old Harp!
(*Mockingly.*) Come on down in hell. Eat up de coal-dust. Drink
in de heat. It's it, see! Act like yuh liked it, yuh better – or
croak yuhself.

PADDY (*with jovial defiance*). To the divil wid it! I'll not report
this watch. Let thim log me and be damned. I'm no slave the
like of you. I'll be sittin' here at me ease, and drinking, and
thinking, and dreaming dreams.

YANK (*contemptuously*). T'inkin' and dreamin', what'll that get
yuh? What's t'inkin' got to do wit it? We move, don't we?
Speed, ain't it? Fog, dat's all you stand for. But we drive trou
dat, don't we? We split dat up and smash trou – twenty-five
knots a' hour! (*Turns his back on PADDY scornfully.*) Aw, yuh
make me sick! Yuh don't belong! (*He strides out the door in rear.
PADDY hums to himself, blinking drowsily.*)

Curtain.

Scene Two

Scene. Two days out. A section of the promenade deck. MILDRED
DOUGLAS *and her aunt are discovered reclining in deck-chairs. The
former is a girl of twenty, slender, delicate, with a pale, pretty face
marred by a self-conscious expression of disdainful superiority. She looks
fretful, nervous and discontented, bored by her own anaemia. Her aunt is
a pompous and proud – and fat – old lady. She is a type even to the
point of a double chin and lorgnettes. She is dressed pretentiously, as if
afraid her face alone would never indicate her position in life.*
MILDRED *is dressed all in white.*

*The impression to be conveyed by this scene is one of the beautiful, vivid
life of the sea all about – sunshine on the deck in a great flood, the fresh
sea wind blowing across it. In the midst of this, these two, incongruous,
artificial figures, inert and disharmonious, the elder like a grey lump of
dough touched up with rouge, the younger looking as if the vitality of her
stock had been sapped before she was conceived, so that she is the*

expression not of its life energy but merely of the artificialities that energy had won for itself in the spending.

MILDRED (*looking up with affected dreaminess*). How the black smoke swirls back against the sky! Is it not beautiful?

AUNT (*without looking up*). I dislike smoke of any kind.

MILDRED. My great-grandmother smoked a pipe – a clay pipe.

AUNT (*ruffling*). Vulgar!

MILDRED. She was too distant a relative to be vulgar. Time mellows pipes.

AUNT (*pretending boredom but irritated*). Did the sociology you took up at college teach you that – to play the ghoul on every possible occasion, excavating old bones? Why not let your great-grandmother rest in her grave?

MILDRED (*dreamily*). With her pipe beside her – puffing in Paradise.

AUNT (*with spite*). Yes, you are a natural born ghoul. You are even getting to look like one, my dear.

MILDRED (*in a passionless tone*). I detest you, aunt. (*Looking at her critically.*) Do you know what you remind me of? Of a cold pork pudding against a background of linoleum tablecloth in the kitchen of a – but the possibilities are wearisome. (*She closes her eyes.*)

AUNT (*with a bitter laugh*). Merci for your candour. But since I am and must be your chaperone – in appearance, at least – let us patch up some sort of armed truce. For my part you are quite free to indulge any pose of eccentricity that beguiles you – as long as you observe the amenities –

MILDRED (*drawling*). The inanities?

AUNT (*going on as if she hadn't heard*). After exhausting the morbid thrills of social service work on New York's East Side – how they must have hated you, by the way, the poor that you made so much poorer in their own eyes! – you are now bent on making your slumming international. Well, I hope Whitechapel will provide the needed nerve tonic. Do not ask me to chaperone you there, however. I told your father I would not. I loathe deformity. We will hire an army of detectives and you may investigate everything – they allow you to see.

MILDRED (*protesting with a trace of genuine earnestness*). Please do not mock at my attempts to discover how the other half lives.

Give me credit for some sort of groping sincerity in that at least. I would like to help them. I would like to be some use in the world. Is it my fault I don't know how? I would like to be sincere, to touch life somewhere. (*With weary bitterness.*) But I'm afraid I have neither the vitality nor integrity. All that was burnt out in our stock before I was born. Grandfather's blast furnaces, flaming to the sky, melting steel, making millions -- then father keeping those home fires burning, making more millions – and little me at the tail-end of it all. I'm a waste product in the Bessemer process – like the millions. Or rather, I inherit the acquired trait of the by-product, wealth, but none of the energy, none of the strength of the steel that made it. I am sired by gold and damned by it, as they say at the race track – damned in more ways than one. (*She laughs mirthlessly.*)

AUNT (*unimpressed – superciliously*). You seem to be going in for sincerity today. It isn't becoming to you, really – except as an obvious pose. Be as artificial as you are, I advise. There's a sort of sincerity in that, you know. And, after all, you must confess you like that better.

MILDRED (*again affected and bored*). Yes, I suppose I do. Pardon me for my outburst. When a leopard complains of its spots, it must sound rather grotesque. (*In a mocking tone.*) Purr, little leopard. Purr, scratch, tear, kill, gorge yourself and be happy – only stay in the jungle where your spots are camouflage. In a cage they make you conspicuous.

AUNT. I don't know what you are talking about.

MILDRED. It would be rude to talk about anything to you. Let's just talk. (*She looks at her wrist watch.*) Well, thank goodness, it's about time for them to come for me. That ought to give me a new thrill, aunt.

AUNT (*affectedly troubled*). You don't mean to say you're really going? The dirt – the heat must be frightful –

MILDRED. Grandfather started as a puddler. I should have inherited an immunity to heat that would make a salamander shiver. It will be fun to put it to the test.

AUNT. But don't you have to have the captain's – or some one's – permission to visit the stokehole?

MILDRED (*with a triumphant smile*). I have it – both his and the chief engineer's. Oh, they didn't want to at first, in spite of my social service credentials. They didn't seem a bit anxious that I should investigate how the other half lives and works on a ship.

So I had to tell them that my father, the president of Nazareth Steel, chairman of the board of directors of this line, had told me it would be all right.

AUNT. He didn't.

MILDRED. How naïve age makes one! But I said he did, aunt. I even said he had given me a letter to them – which I had lost. And they were afraid to take the chance that I might be lying. (*Excitedly.*) So it's ho! for the stokehole. The second engineer is to escort me. (*Looking at her watch again.*) It's time. And here he comes, I think.

The SECOND ENGINEER *enters. He is a fine-looking man of thirty-five or so. He stops before the two and tips his cap, visibly embarrassed and ill at ease.*

SECOND ENGINEER. Miss Douglas?

MILDRED. Yes. (*Throwing off her rugs and getting to her feet.*) Are we all ready to start?

SECOND ENGINEER. In just a second, ma'am. I'm waiting for the Fourth. He's coming along.

MILDRED (*with a scornful smile*). You don't care to shoulder this responsibility alone, is that it?

SECOND ENGINEER (*forcing a smile*). Two are better than one. (*Disturbed by her eyes, glances out to sea – blurts out.*) A fine day we're having.

MILDRED. Is it?

SECOND ENGINEER. A nice warm breeze –

MILDRED. It feels cold to me.

SECOND ENGINEER. But it's hot enough in the sun –

MILDRED. Not hot enough for me. I don't like Nature. I was never athletic.

SECOND ENGINEER (*forcing a smile*). Well, you'll find it hot enough where you're going.

MILDRED. Do you mean hell?

SECOND ENGINEER (*flabbergasted, decides to laugh*). Ho-ho! No, I mean the stokehole.

MILDRED. My grandfather was a puddler. He played with boiling steel.

SECOND ENGINEER (*all at sea – uneasily*). Is that so? Hum,

you'll excuse me, ma'am, but are you intending to wear that dress?

MILDRED. Why not?

SECOND ENGINEER. You'll likely rub against oil and dirt. It can't be helped.

MILDRED. It doesn't matter. I have lots of white dresses.

SECOND ENGINEER. I have an old coat you might throw over –

MILDRED. I have fifty dresses like this. I will throw this one into the sea when I come back. That ought to wash it clean, don't you think?

SECOND ENGINEER (*doggedly*). There's ladders to climb down that are none too clean – and dark alley-ways –

MILDRED. I will wear this very dress and none other.

SECOND ENGINEER. No offence meant. It's none of my business. I was only warning you –

MILDRED. Warning? That sounds thrilling.

SECOND ENGINEER (*looking down the deck – with a sigh of relief*). There's the Fourth now. He's waiting for us. If you'll come –

MILDRED. Go on. I'll follow you. (*He goes.* MILDRED *turns a mocking smile on her aunt.*) An oaf – but a handsome, virile oaf.

AUNT (*scornfully*). Poser!

MILDRED. Take care. He said there were dark alley-ways –

AUNT (*in the same tone*). Poser!

MILDRED (*biting her lips angrily*). You are right. But would that my millions were not so anaemically chaste!

AUNT. Yes, for a fresh pose I have no doubt you would drag the name of Douglas in the gutter!

MILDRED. From which it sprang. Goodbye, aunt. Don't pray too hard that I may fall into the fiery furnace.

AUNT. Poser!

MILDRED (*viciously*). Old hag! (*She slaps her aunt insultingly across the face and walks off, laughing gaily.*)

AUNT (*screams after her*). I said poser!

Curtain.

Scene Three

Scene. The stokehole. In the rear, the dimly-outlined bulks of the furnaces and boilers. High overhead one hanging electric bulb sheds just enough light through the murky air laden with coal-dust to pile up masses of shadows everywhere. A line of men, stripped to the waist, is before the furnace doors. They bend over, looking neither to right nor left, handling their shovels as if they were part of their bodies, with a strange, awkward, swinging rhythm. They use the shovels to throw open the furnace doors. Then from these fiery round holes in the black a flood of terrific light and heat pours full upon the men who are outlined in silhouette in the crouching, inhuman attitudes of chained gorillas. The men shovel with a rhythmic motion, swinging as on a pivot from the coal which lies in heaps on the floor behind to hurl it into the flaming mouths before them. There is a tumult of noise – the brazen clang of the furnace doors as they are flung open or slammed shut, the grating, teeth-gritting grind of steel against steel, of crunching coal. This clash of sounds stuns one's ears with its rending dissonance. But there is order in it, rhythm, a mechanical, regulated recurrence, a tempo. And rising above all, making the air hum with the quiver of liberated energy, the roar of leaping flames in the furnaces, the monotonous throbbing beat of the engines.

As the curtain rises, the furnace doors are shut. The men are taking a breathing spell. One or two are arranging the coal behind them, pulling it into more accessible heaps. The others can be dimly made out leaning on their shovels in relaxed attitudes of exhaustion.

PADDY (*from somewhere in the line – plaintively*). Yerra, will this divil's own watch nivir end? Me back is broke. I'm destroyed entirely.

YANK (*from the centre of the line – with exuberant scorn*). Aw, yuh make me sick! Lie down and croak, why don't yuh? Always beefin', dat's you! Say, dis is a cinch! Dis was made for me! It's my meat, get me! (*A whistle is blown – a thin, shrill note from somewhere overhead in the darkness. YANK curses without resentment.*) Dere's de damn engineer crackin' de whip. He tinks we're loafin'.

PADDY (*vindictively*). God stiffen him!

YANK (*in an exultant tone of command*). Come on, youse guys! Git into de game! She's gittin' hungry! Pile some grub in her! Trow it into her belly! Come on now, all of youse! Open her up! (*At this last all the men, who have followed his movements of getting into position, throw open their furnace doors with a deafening clang. The fiery light floods over their shoulders as they bend round for the coal.*

*Rivulets of sooty sweat have traced maps on their backs. The enlarged
muscles form bunches of high light and shadow.*)

YANK (*chanting a count as he shovels without seeming effort*). One –
two – three – (*His voice rising exultantly in the joy of battle.*) Dat's
de stuff! Let her have it! All togedder now! Sling it into her!
Let her ride! Shoot de piece now! Call de toin on her! Drive
her into it! Feel her move! Watch her smoke! Speed, dat's her
middle name! Give her coal, youse guys! Coal, dat's her booze!
Drink it up, baby! Let's see yuh sprint! Dig in and gain a lap!
Dere she go-o-es. (*This last in the chanting formula of the gallery
gods at the six-day bike race. He slams his furnace door shut. The
others do likewise with as much unison as their wearied bodies will
permit. The effect is of one fiery eye after another being blotted out with
a series of accompanying bangs.*)

PADDY (*groaning*). Me back is broke. I'm bate out – bate – (*There
is a pause. Then the inexorable whistle sounds again from the dim
regions above the electric light. There is a growl of cursing rage from
all sides.*)

YANK (*shaking his fist upwards – contemptuously*). Take it easy dere,
you! Who d'yuh tinks runnin' dis game, me or you? When I git
ready, we move. Not before! When I git ready, get me!

VOICES (*approvingly*).
That's the stuff!
Yank tal him, py golly!
Yank ain't affeerd.
Goot poy, Yank!
Give him hell!
Tell 'im 'e's a bloody swine!
Bloody slave-driver!

YANK (*contemptuously*). He ain't got no noive. He's yellow, get
me? All de engineers is yellow. Dey got streaks a mile wide. Aw,
to hell wit him! Let's move, youse guys. We had a rest. Come
on, she needs it! Give her pep! It ain't for him. Him and his
whistle, dey don't belong. But we belong, see! We gotter feed
de baby! Come on!

*He turns and flings his furnace door open. They all follow his lead. At
this instant the* SECOND *and* FOURTH ENGINEER *enter from
the darkness on the left with* MILDRED *between them. She starts,
turns paler, her pose is crumbling, she shivers with fright in spite of the
blazing heat, but forces herself to leave the engineers and take a few
steps nearer the men. She is right behind* YANK. *All this happens
quickly while the men have their backs turned.*

Come on, youse guys! (*He is turning to get coal when the whistle sounds again in a peremptory irritating note. This drives* YANK *into a sudden fury. While the other men have turned full around and stopped dumbfounded by the spectacle of* MILDRED *standing there in her white dress,* YANK *does not turn far enough to see her. Besides, his head is thrown back, he blinks upward through the murk trying to find the owner of the whistle, he brandishes his shovel murderously over his head in one hand, pounding on his chest, gorilla-like, with the other, shouting.*) Toin off dat whistle! Come down outa dere, yuh yellow, brass-buttoned, Belfast scut, yuh! Come down and I'll knock her brains out! Yuh lousey, stinkin', yellow mut of a Catholic-moiderin' bastard! Come down and I'll moider yuh! Pullin' dat whistle on me, huh? I'll show yuh! I'll crash yer skull in! I'll drive yer teet' down yer troat! I'll slam yer nose trou de back of yer yead! I'll cut yer guts out for a nickel, yuh lousey boob, yuh dirty, crummy, muck-eatin' son of a – (*Suddenly he becomes conscious of all the other men staring at something directly behind his back. He whirls defensively with a snarling, murderous growl, crouching to spring, his lips drawn back over his teeth, his small eyes gleaming ferociously. He sees* MILDRED, *like a white apparition in the full light from the open furnace doors. He glares into her eyes, turned to stone. As for her, during his speech she has listened, paralysed with horror, terror, her whole personality crushed, beaten in, collapsed, by the terrific impact of this unknown, abysmal brutality, naked and shameless. As she looks at his gorilla face, as his eyes bore into hers, she utters a low, choking cry and shrinks away from him, putting both hands up before her eyes to shut out the sight of his face, to protect her own. This startles* YANK *to a reaction. His mouth falls open, his eyes grow bewildered.*)

MILDRED (*about to faint – to the* ENGINEERS, *who now have her one by each arm – whimperingly*). Take me away! Oh, the filthy beast! (*She faints. They carry her quickly back, disappearing in the darkness at the left, rear. An iron door clangs shut. Rage and bewildered fury rush back on* YANK. *He feels himself insulted in some unknown fashion in the very heart of his pride. He roars:* God damn yuh! *And hurls his shovel after them at the door which has just closed. It hits the steel bulkhead with a clang and falls clattering on the steel floor. From overhead the whistle sounds again, in a long, angry, insistent command.*)

Curtain.

Scene Four

*Scene. The firemen's forecastle. YANK's watch has just come off duty
and had dinner. Their faces and bodies shine from a soap and water
scrubbing, but around their eyes, where a hasty dousing does not touch,
the coal-dust sticks like black make-up, giving them a queer, sinister
expression. YANK has not washed either face or body. He stands out in
contrast to them, a blackened, brooding figure. He is seated forward on a
bench in the exact attitude of Rodin's 'The Thinker.' The others, most of
them smoking pipes, are staring at YANK half-apprehensively, as if
fearing an outburst; half-amusedly, as if they saw a joke somewhere that
tickled them.*

VOICES.
   He ain't ate nothin'.
   Py golly, a fallar gat gat grub in him.
   Divil a lie.
   Yank feeda da fire, no feeda da face.
   Ha-ha.
   He ain't even washed hisself.
   He's forgot.
   Hey, Yank, you forgot to wash.

YANK (*sullenly*). Forgot nothin'! To hell wit washin'.

VOICES.
   It'll stick to you.
   It'll get under your skin.
   Give yer the bleedin' itch, that's wot.
   It makes spots on you – like a leopard.
   Like a piebald nigger, you mean.
   Better wash up, Yank.
   You sleep better.
   Wash up, Yank.
   Wash up! Wash up!

YANK (*resentfully*). Aw say, youse guys. Lemme alone. Can't
   youse see I'm tryin' to tink?

ALL (*repeating the word after him as one with cynical mockery*). Think!
   (*The word has a brazen, metallic quality as if their throats were
   phonograph horns. It is followed by a chorus of hard, barking
   laughter*).

YANK (*springing to his feet and glaring at them belligerently*). Yes,
   tink! Tink, dat's what I said! What about it! (*They are silent,
   puzzled by his sudden resentment at what used to be one of his jokes.
   YANK sits down again in the same attitude of 'The Thinker.'*)

VOICES.
> Leave him alone.
> He's got a grouch on.
> Why wouldn't he?

PADDY (*with a wink at the others*). Sure I know what's the matther.
'Tis aisy to see. He's fallen in love, I'm telling you.

ALL (*repeating the word after him as one with cynical mockery*). Love!
(*The word has a brazen, metallic quality as if their throats were
phonograph horns. It is followed by a chorus of hard, barking
laughter*).

YANK (*with a contemptuous snort*). Love, hell! Hate, dat's what. I've
fallen in hate, get me?

PADDY (*philosophically*). 'Twould take a wise man to tell one from
the other. (*With a bitter, ironical scorn, increasing as he goes on.*)
But I'm telling you it's love that's in it. Sure what else but love
for us poor bastes in the stokehole would be bringing a fine
lady, dressed like a white quane, down a mile of ladders and
steps to be havin' a look at us? (*A growl of anger goes up from all
sides.*)

LONG (*jumping on a bench -- hectically*). Hinsultin' us! Hinsultin'
us, the bloody cow! And them bloody engineers! What right 'as
they got to be exhibitin' us 's if we was bleedin' monkeys in a
menagerie? Did we sign for hinsults to our dignity as 'onest
workers? Is that in the ship's articles? You kin bloody well bet it
ain't! But I knows why they done it. I arsked a deck steward 'o
she was and 'e told me. 'Er old man's a bleedin' millionaire, a
bloody Capitalist! 'E's got enuf bloody gold to sink this bleedin'
ship! 'E makes arf the bloody steel in the world! 'E owns this
bloody boat! And you and me, comrades, we're 'is slaves! And
the skipper and mates and engineers, they're 'is slaves! And
she's 'is bloody daughter and we're all 'er slaves, too! And she
gives 'er orders as 'ow she wants to see the bloody animals
below decks and down they takes 'er! (*There is a roar of rage from
all sides.*)

YANK (*blinking at him, bewildered*). Say! Wait a moment! Is all dat
straight goods?

LONG. Straight as string! The bleedin' steward as waits on 'em, 'e
told me about 'er. And what're we goin' ter do, I arsks yer?
'Ave we got ter swaller 'er hinsults like dogs? It ain't in the
ship's articles. I tell yer we got a case. We kin go ter law –

YANK (*with abysmal contempt*). Hell! Law!

ALL (*repeating the word after him as one with cynical mockery*). Law!
(*The word has a brazen, metallic quality as if their throats were
phonograph horns. It is followed by a chorus of hard, barking
laughter.*)

LONG (*feeling the ground slipping from under his feet – desperately*).
As voters and citizens we kin force the bloody Governments –

YANK (*with abysmal contempt*). Hell! Governments!

ALL (*repeating the word after him as one with cynical mockery*).
Governments! (*The word has a brazen, metallic quality as if their
throats were phonograph horns. It is followed by a chorus of hard,
barking laughter.*)

LONG (*hysterically*). We're free and equal in the sight of God –

YANK (*with abysmal contempt*). Hell! God!

ALL (*repeating the word after him as one with cynical mockery*). God!
(*The word has a brazen, metallic quality as if their throats were
phonograph horns. It is followed by a chorus of hard, barking
laughter.*)

YANK. (*witheringly*). Aw, join de Salvation Army!

ALL. Sit down! Shut up! Damn fool! Sea-lawyer! (LONG *slinks
back out of sight.*)

PADDY (*continuing the trend of his thoughts as if he had never been
interrupted – bitterly*). And there she was standing behind us, and
the Second pointing at us like a man you'd hear in a circus
would be saying: In this cage is a queerer kind of baboon than
ever you'd find in darkest Africy. We roast them in their own
sweat – and be damned if you won't hear some of thim saying
they like it! (*He glances scornfully at* YANK.)

YANK (*with a bewildered, uncertain growl*). Aw!

PADDY. And there was Yank roarin' curses and turning round
wid his shovel to brain her – and she looked at him, and him at
her –

YANK (*slowly*). She was all white. I tought she was a ghost. Sure.

PADDY (*with heavy, biting sarcasm*). 'Twas love at first sight, divil a
doubt of it! If you'd seen the endearin' look on her pale mug
when she shrivelled away with her hands over her eyes to shut
out the sight of him! Sure, 'twas as if she'd seen a great hairy
ape escaped from the Zoo!

YANK (*stung – with a growl of rage*). Aw!

PADDY. And the loving way Yank heaved his shovel at the skull of her, only she was out the door! (*A grin breaking over his face.*) 'Twas touching, I'm telling you! It put the touch of home, swate home in the stokehole. (*There is a roar of laughter from all.*)

YANK (*glaring at* PADDY *menacingly*). Aw, choke dat off, see!

PADDY (*not heeding him – to the others*). And her grabbin' at the Second's arm for protection. (*With a grotesque imitation of a woman's voice.*) Kiss me, Engineer dear, for it's dark down here and me old man's in Wall Street making money! Hug me tight, darlin', for I'm afeerd in the dark and me mother's on deck makin' eyes at the skipper! (*Another roar of laugher.*)

YANK (*threateningly*). Say! What yuh tryin' to do, kid me, yuh old Harp?

PADDY. Divil a bit! Ain't I wishin' myself you'd brained her?

YANK (*fiercely*). I'll brain her! I'll brain her yet, wait'n see! (*Coming over to* PADDY *– slowly.*) Say, is dat what she called me – a hairy ape?

PADDY. She looked it at you if she didn't say the word itself.

YANK (*grinning horribly*). Hairy ape, huh? Sure! Dat's de way she looked at me, aw right. Hairy ape! So dat's me, huh? (*Bursting into rage – as if she were still in front of him.*) Yuh skinny tart! Yuh white-faced slut, yuh! I'll show yuh who's a ape! (*Turning to the others, bewilderment seizing him again.*) Say, youse guys. I was bawlin' him out for pullin' de whistle on us. You heard me. And den I seen youse lookin' at somep'n and I tought he'd sneaked down to come up in back of me, and I hopped round to knock him dead wit de shovel. And dere she was wit de light on her! Christ, yuh could a-pushed me over with a finger! I was scared, get me? Sure! I tought she was a ghost, see? She was all in white like dey wrap around stiffs. You seen her. Kin yuh blame me? She didn't belong, dat's what. And den when I come to and seen it was a real skoit and seen de way she was lookin' at me – like Paddy said – Christ, I was sore, get me? I don't stand for dat stuff from nobody. And I flung de shovel – on'y she'd beat it. (*Furiously.*) I wished it'd banged her! I wished it'd knocked her block off!

LONG. And be 'anged for murder or 'lectrocuted? She ain't bleedin' well worth it.

YANK. I don't give a damn what! I'd be square wit her, wouldn't I! Tink I wanter let her put somep'n over on me? Tink I'm

going to let her git away wit dat stuff? Yuh don't know me! No
one ain't never put nothin' over on me and got away wit it, see!
– not dat kind of stuff – no guy and no skoit neither! I'll fix
her! Maybe she'll come down again –

VOICE. No chance, Yank. You scared her out of a year's growth.

YANK. I scared her? Why de hell should I scare her? Who de
hell is she? Ain't she de same as me? Hairy ape, huh? (*With his
old confident bravado.*) I'll show her I'm better'n her, if she on'y
knew it. I belong and she don't, see! I move and she's dead!
Twenty-five knots a hour, dats me! Dat carries her, but I make
dat. She's on'y baggage. Sure! (*Again bewildered.*) But, Christ,
she was funny lookin'! Did yuh pipe her hands? White and
skinny. Yuh could see de bones trough 'em. And her mush, dat
was dead white, too. And her eyes, dey was like dey'd seen a
ghost. Me, dat was! Sure! Hairy Ape! Ghost, huh? Look at dat
arm! (*He extends his right arm, swelling out the great muscles.*) I
could a-took her wit dat, wit' just my little finger even, and
broke her in two. (*Again, bewildered.*) Say, who is dat skoit, huh?
What is she? What's she come from? Who made her? Who give
her de noive to look at me like dat? Dis ting's got my goat
right. I don't get her. She's new to me. What does a skoit like
her mean, huh? She don't belong, get me! I can't see her. (*With
growing anger.*) But one ting I'm wise to, aw right, aw right!
Youse all kin bet your shoits I'll git even wit her. I'll show her if
she tinks she – She grinds de organ and I'm on de string, huh?
I'll fix her! Let her come down again and I'll fling her in de
furnace! She'll move den! She won't shiver at nothin', den!
Speed, dat'll be her! She'll belong den! (*He grins horribly.*)

PADDY. She'll never come. She's had her belly-full, I'm telling
you. She'll be in bed now, I'm thinking, wid ten doctors and
nurses feedin' her salts to clean the fear out of her.

YANK (*enraged*). Yuh tink I made her sick, too, do yuh? Just
lookin' at me, huh? Hairy ape, huh? (*In a frenzy of rage.*) I'll fix
her! I'll tell her where to git off! She'll git down on her knees
and take it back or I'll bust de face offen her! (*Shaking one fist
upward and beating on his chest with the other.*) I'll find yuh! I'm
comin', d'you hear? I'll fix yuh, God damn yuh! (*He makes a
rush for the door.*)

VOICES.
  Stop him!
  He'll get shot!
  He'll murder her!

Trip him up!
Hold him!
He's gone crazy!
Gott, he's strong!
Hold him down!
Look out for a kick!
Pin his arms!

They have all piled on him and, after a fierce struggle, by sheer weight of numbers have borne him to the floor just inside the door.

PADDY (*who has remained detached*). Kape him down, till he's cooled off. (*Scornfully.*) Yerra, Yank, you're a great fool. Is it payin' attention at all you are to the like of that skinny sow widout one drop of rale blood in her?

YANK (*frenziedly, from the bottom of the heap*). She done me doit! She done me doit, didn't she? I'll git square wit her! I'll get her some way! Gif offen me, youse guys! Lemme up! I'll show her who's a ape!

Curtain.

Scene Five

Scene. Three weeks later. A corner of Fifth Avenue on a fine Sunday morning. A general atmosphere of clean, well-tidied, wide street; a flood of mellow, tempered sunshine; gentle, genteel breezes. In the rear, the show windows of two shops, a jewellery establishment on the corner, a furrier's next to it. Here the adornments of extreme wealth are tantalizingly displayed. The jeweller's window is gaudy with glittering, diamonds, emeralds, rubies, pearls, etc., fashioned in ornate tiaras, crowns, necklaces, collars, etc. From each piece hangs an enormous rag from which a dollar sign and numerals in intermittent electric lights wink out the incredible prices. The same in the furrier's. Rich furs of all varieties hang there bathed in a downpour of artificial light. The general effect is of a background of magnificence cheapened and made grotesque by commercialism, a background in tawdry disharmony with the clear light and sunshine on the street itself.

Up the side street YANK and LONG come swaggering. LONG is dressed in shore clothes, wears a black tie and cloth cap. YANK is in his dirty dungarees. A fireman's cap with black peak is cocked defiantly on the side of his head. He has not shaved for days, and around his fierce, resentful eyes — as around those of LONG to a lesser degree — the black smudge of coal-dust still sticks like make-up. They hesitate and stand together at the corner, swaggering, looking about them with a forced, defiant contempt.

LONG (*indicating it all with an oratorical gesture*). Well, 'ere we are. Fif' Avenoo. This 'ere's their bleedin' private lane, as yer might say. (*Bitterly.*) We're trespassers 'ere. Proletarians keep orf the grass!

YANK (*dully*). I don't see no grass, yuh boob. (*Staring at the pavement.*) Clean, ain't it? Yuh could eat a fried egg offen it. The white wings got some job sweepin' dis up. (*Looking up and down the avenue – surlily.*) Where's all the white-collar stiffs yuh said was here – and de skoits – *her* kind?

LONG. In church, blarst 'em! Arskin' Jesus to give 'em more money.

YANK. Choich, huh? I useter go to choich onct – sure – when I was a kid. Me old man and woman, dey made me. Dey never went demselves, dough. Always got too big a head on Sunday mornin', dat was dem. (*With a grin.*) Dey was scrappers for fair, bot' of dem. On Satiday nights when dey bot' got a skinful dey could put up a bout oughter been staged at de Garden. When dey got trough dere wasn't a chair or table wit a leg under it. Or else dey bot' jumped on me for somep'n. Dat was where I loined to take punishment. (*With a grin and a swagger.*) I'm a chip offen de old block, get me?

LONG. Did yer old man follow the sea?

YANK. Naw. Worked along shore. I runned away when me old lady croaked wit de tremens. I helped at truckin' and in de market. Den I shipped in de stokehole. Sure. Dat belongs. De rest was nothin'. (*Looking around him.*) I ain't never seen dis before. De Brooklyn waterfront, dat was where I was dragged up. (*Taking a deep breath.*) Dis ain't so bad at dat, huh?

LONG. Not bad? Well, we pays for it wiv our bloody sweat, if yer wants to know!

YANK (*with sudden angry disgust*). Aw, hell! I don't see no one, see – like her. All dis gives me a pain. It don't belong. Say, ain't dere a backroom around dis dump? Let's go shoot a ball. All dis is too clean and quiet and dolled-up, get me! It gives me a pain.

LONG. Wait and yer'll bloody well see –

YANK. I don't wait for no one. I keep on de move. Say, what

yuh drag me up here for, anyway? Tryin' to kid me, yuh simp, yuh?

LONG. Yer wants to get back at her, don't yer? That's what yer been sayin' every bloomin' 'our since she hinsulted yer.

YANK (*vehemently*). Sure ting I do! Didn't I try to git even wit her in Southampton? Didn't I sneak on de dock and wait for her by de gangplank? I was goin' to spit in her pale mug, see! Sure, right in her pop-eyes! Dat would a-made me even, see? But no chanct. Dere was a whole army of plain clothes bulls around. Dey spotted me and gimme de rush. I never seen her. But I'll git square wit her yet, you watch! (*Furiously.*) De lousey tart! She tinks she kin get away wit moider – but not wit me! I'll fix her! I'll tink of a way!

LONG (*as disgusted as he dares to be*). Ain't that why I brought yer up 'ere – to show yer? Yer been lookin' at this 'ere 'ole affair wrong. Yer been actin' an talkin's if it was all a bleedin' personal matter between yer and that bloody cow. I wants to convince yer she was on'y a representative of 'er clarss. I wants to awaken yer bloody clarss consciousness. Then yer'll see it's 'er clarss yer've got to fight, not 'er alone. There's a 'ole mob of 'em like 'er, Gawd blind 'em!

YANK (*spitting on his hands – belligerently*). De more de merrier when I gits started. Bring on de gang!

LONG. Yer'll see 'em in arf a mo', when that church lets out. (*He turns and sees the window display in the two stores for the first time.*) Blimey! Look at that, will yer? (*They both walk back and stand looking in the jeweller's. LONG flies into a fury.*) Just look at this 'ere bloomin' mess! Just look at it! Look at the bleedin' prices on 'em – more'n our 'old bloody stokehole makes in ten voyages sweatin' in 'ell! And they – her and her bloody clarss – buys 'em for toys to dangle on 'em! One of these 'ere would buy grub for a starvin' family for a year!

YANK. Aw, cut de sob stuf! T' hell wit de starvin' family! Yuh'll be passin' de hat to me next. (*With naïve admiration.*) Say, dem tings is pretty, huh? Bet yuh dey'd hock for a piece of change aw right. (*Then turning away, bored.*) But, aw hell, what good are dey? Let her have 'em. Dey don't belong no more'n she does. (*With a gesture of sweeping the jeweller's into oblivion.*) All dat don't count, get me?

LONG (*who has moved to the furrier's – indignantly.*) And I s'pose this 'ere don't count neither – skins of poor 'armless animals slaughtered so as 'er and 'ers can keep their bleedin' noses warm!

YANK (*who has been staring at something inside – with queer excitement*). Take a slant at dat! Give it de once-over! Monkey fur – two t'ousand bucks! (*Bewildered.*) Is dat straight goods – monkey fur? What de hell –

LONG (*bitterly.*) It's straight enuf. (*With grim humour.*) They wouldn't bloody well pay that for a 'airy ape's skin – no, nor for the 'ole livin' ape with all 'is 'ead, and body, and soul thrown in!

YANK (*clenching his fists, his face growing pale with rage as if the skin in the window were a personal insult*). Trowin' it up in my face! Christ! I'll fix her!

LONG (*excitedly*). Church is out. 'Ere they come, the bleedin' swine. (*After a glance at* YANK's *glowering face – uneasily.*) Easy goes, Comrade. Keep yer bloomin' temper. Remember force defeats itself. It ain't our weapon. We must impress our demands through peaceful means – the votes of the on-marching proletarians of the bloody world!

YANK (*with abysmal contempt*). Votes, hell! Votes is a joke, see. Votes for women! Let dem do it!

LONG (*still more uneasily*). Calm, now. Treat 'em wiv the proper contempt. Observe the bleedin' parasites, but 'old yer 'orses.

YANK (*angrily*). Git away from me! Yuh're yellow, dat's what. Force, dat's me! De punch, dat's me every time, see!

The crowd from church enter from the right, sauntering slowly and affectedly, their heads held stiffly up, looking neither to right nor left, talking in toneless, simpering voices. The women are rouged, calcimined, dyed, overdressed to the nth degree. The men are in tail coats, tall hats, spats, canes, etc. A procession of gaudy marionettes, yet with something of the relentless horror of Frankensteins in their detached, mechanical unawareness.

VOICES.
   Dear Doctor Caiaphas! He is so sincere!
   What was the sermon? I dozed off.
   About the radicals, my dear – and the false doctrines that are being preached.
   We must organize a hundred per cent American bazaar.
   And let everyone contribute one one-hundredth per cent of their income tax.
   What an original idea!

We can devote the proceeds to rehabilitate the veil of the temple. But that has been done so many times.

YANK (*glaring from one to the other of them – with an insulting snort of corn*). Huh! Huh!

Without seeming to see him, they make wide detours to avoid the spot where he stands in the middle of the pavement.

LONG (*frightened*). Keep yer bloomin' mouth shut, I tells yer.

YANK (*viciously*). G'wan! Tell it to Sweeney! (*He swaggers away and deliberately lurches into a top-hatted gentleman, then glares at him pugnaciously.*) Say, who d'yuh tink yuh're bumpin'? Tink yuh own de oith?

GENTLEMAN (*coldly and affectedly*). I beg your pardon. (*He has not looked at* YANK *and passes on without a glance, leaving him bewildered.*)

LONG (*rushing up and grabbing* YANK's *arm*). 'Ere! Come away! This wasn't what I meant. Yer'll 'ave the bloody coppers down on us.

YANK (*savagely – giving him a push that sends him sprawling*). G'wan!

LONG (*picks himself up – hysterically*). I'll pop orf then. This ain't what I meant. And whatever 'appens, yer can't blame me. (*He slinks off left.*)

YANK. T' hell wit youse! (*He approaches a lady – with a vicious grin and a smirking wink.*) Hallo, Kiddo. How's every little ting? Got anyting on for tonight? I know an old boiler down to de docks we kin crawl into. (*The lady stalks by without a look, without a change of pace.* YANK *turns to others – insultingly.*) Holy smokes, what a mug! Go hide yuhself before de horses shy at yuh. Gee, pipe de heinie on dat one! Say, youse, yuh look like de stoin of a ferryboat. Paint and powder! All dolled up to kill! Yuh look like stiffs laid out for de boneyard! Aw, g'wan, de lot of youse! Yuh give me de eyeache. Yuh don't belong, get me! Look at me, why don't youse dare? I belong, dat's me! (*Pointing to a skyscraper across the street which is in process of construction – with bravado.*) See dat building goin' up dere? See de steel work? Steel, dat's me! Youse guys live on it and tink yuh're somep'n. But I'm *in* it, see! I'm de hoistin' engine dat makes it go up! I'm it – de inside and bottom of it! Sure! I'm steel and steam and smoke and de rest of it! It moves – speed – twenty-five stories up – and me at de top and bottom – movin'! Youse

simps don't move. Yuh're on'y dolls I winds up to see'm spin.
Yuh're de garbage, get me – de leavin's – de ashes we dump
over de side! Now, what a-yuh got to say? (*But as they seem
neither to see nor hear him, he flies into a fury*). Pigs! Tarts! Bitches!
(*He turns in a rage on the men, bumping viciously into them but not
jarring them the least bit. Rather it is he who recoils after each
collision. He keeps growling.*) Git off de oith! G'wan! Look where
yuh're goin', can't yuh? Git out a-here! Fight, why don't huh?
Put up yer mits! Don't be a dog! Fight, or I'll knock yuh dead!
(*But, without seeming to see him, they all answer with mechanical,
affected politeness:*) I beg your pardon. (*Then at a cry from one of
the women, they all scurry to the furrier's window.*)

THE WOMAN (*ecstatically, with a gasp of delight*). Monkey fur!
(*The whole crowd of men and women chorus after her in the same tone
of affected delight.*) Monkey fur!

YANK (*with a jerk of his head back on his shoulders, as if he had
received a punch full in the face – raging*). I see yuh, all in white! I
see yuh, yuh white-faced tart, yuh! Hairy ape, huh? I'll hairy
ape yuh!

*He bends down and grips at the street kerbing as if to pluck it out and
hurl it. Foiled in this, snarling with passion, he leaps to the lamp-post
on the corner and tries to pull it up for a club. Just at that moment a
bus is heard rumbling up. A fat, high-hatted, spatted gentleman runs
out from the side street. He calls out plaintively:* 'Bus! Bus! Stop
there!' *and runs full tilt into the bending, straining* YANK, *who is
bowled of his balance.*

YANK (*seeing a fight – with a roar of joy as he springs to his feet*). At
last! Bus, huh? I'll bust yuh!

*He lets drive a terrific swing, his fist landing full on the fat
gentleman's face. But the gentleman stands unmoved as if nothing had
happened.*

GENTLEMAN. I beg your pardon. (*Then irritably*). You have
made me lose my bus. (*He claps his hands and begins to scream.*)
Officer! Officer!

*Many police whistles shrill out on the instant, and a whole platoon of
policeman rush in on* YANK *from all sides. He tries to fight, but is
clubbed to the pavement and fallen upon. The crowd at the window
have not moved or noticed this disturbance. The clanging gong of the
patrol wagon approaches with a clamouring din.*

Curtain.

Scene Six

Scene. Night of the following day. A row of cells in the prison in Blackwells Island. The cells extend back diagonally from right front to left rear. They do not stop, but disappear in the dark background as if they ran on, numberless, into infinity. One electric bulb from the low ceiling of the narrow corridor sheds its light through the heavy steel bars of the cell at the extreme front and reveals part of the interior. YANK can be seen within, crouched on the edge of his cot in the attitude of Rodin's 'The Thinker'. His face is spotted with black and blue bruises. A blood-stained bandage is wrapped around his head.

YANK (*suddenly starting as if awakening from a dream, reaches out and shakes the bars – aloud to himself, wonderingly*). Steel. Dis is de Zoo, huh? (*A burst of hard, barking laughter comes from the unseen occupants of the cells, runs back down the tier, and abruptly ceases.*)

VOICES (*mockingly.*)
   The Zoo? That's a new name for this coop – a damn good name!
   Steel, eh? You said a mouthful. This is the old iron house.
   Who is that boob talkin'?
   He's the bloke they brung in out of his head. The bulls had beat him up fierce.

YANK (*dully*). I must a-been dreamin'. I tought I was in a cage at de Zoo – but de apes don't talk, do dey?

VOICES (*with mocking laughter*).
   You're in a cage aw right.
   A coop!
   A pen!
   A sty!
   A kennel! (*Hard laughter – a pause.*)
   Say, guy! Who are you? No, never mind lying. What are you?
   Yes, tell us your sad story. What's your game?
   What did they jug yuh for?

YANK (*dully*). I was a fireman – stokin' on de liners. (*Then with sudden rage, rattling his cell bars.*) I'm a hairy ape, get me? And I'll bust youse all in de jaw if yuh don't lay off kiddin' me.

VOICES.
   Huh! You're a hard-boiled duck, ain't you!
   When you spit, it bounces! (*Laughter.*)
   Aw, can it. He's a regular guy. Ain't you?
   What did he say he was – a ape?

YANK (*defiantly*). Sure ting! Ain't dat what youse all are – apes?
(*A silence. Then a furious rattling of bars from down the corridor.*)

A VOICE (*thick with rage*). I'll show yuh who's a ape, yuh mut!

VOICES.
Sshh! Nix!
Can de noise!
Piano!
You'll have the guard down on us!

YANK (*scornfully*). De guard? Yuh mean de keeper, don't yuh?
(*Angry exclamations from all the cells*).

VOICE (*placatingly*). Aw, don't pay no attention to him. He's off
his nut from the beatin'-up he got. Say, you guy! We're waitin'
to hear what they landed you for – or ain't yuh tellin'?

YANK. Sure, I'll tell youse. Sure! Why de hell not? On'y – youse
won't get me. Nobody gets me but me, see? I started to tell de
Judge and all he says was: 'Toity days to tink it oer.' Tink it
over! Christ, dat's all I been doin' for weeks! (*After a pause.*) I
was tryin' to git even wit some one, see? – some one dat done
me doit.

VOICES (*cynically*).
De old stuff, I bet. Your goil, huh?
Give yuh the double-cross, huh?
That's them every time!
Did yuh beat up de odder guy?

YANK (*disgustedly*). Aw, yuh're all wrong! Sure, dere was a skoit
in it – but not what youse mean, not dat old trip. Dis was a new
kind of skoit. She was dolled up all in white – in de stokehole, I
tought she was a ghost. Sure. (*A pause.*)

VOICES (*whispering.*)
Gee, he's still nutty.
Let him rave. It's fun listenin'.

YANK (*unheeding – groping in his thoughts*). Her hands – dey was
skinny and white like dey wasn't real but painted on somep'n.
Dere was a million miles from me to her – twenty five knots a
hour. She was like some dead ting de cat brung in. Sure, dat's
what. She didn't belong. She belonged in de wndow of a toy
store, or on de top of a garbage can, see! Sure! (*He breaks out
angrily.*) But would yuh believe it, she had de noive to do me
doit. She lamped me like she was seein' somep'n broke loose
from de menagerie. Christ, yuh'd oughter seen her eyes! (*He

rattles the bars of his cell furiously.) But I'll get back at her yet, you watch! And if I can't find her, I'll take it out on de gang she runs wit. I'm wise to where dey hangs out now. I'll show her who belongs! I'll show her who's in de move and who ain't. You watch my smoke!

VOICES (*serious and joking*).
Dat's de talkin'!
Take her for all she's got!
What was this dame, anyway? Who was she, eh?

YANK. I dunno. First cabin stiff. Her old man's a millionaire, dey seys – name of Douglas.

VOICES.
Douglas? That's the President of the Steel Trust, I bet.
Sure. I seen his mug in de papers.
He's filthy with dough.

VOICE. Hey, feller, take a tip from me. If you want to get back at that dame, you better join the Wobblies. You'll get some action then.

YANK. Wobblies? What de hell's dat?

VOICE. Ain't you ever heard of the I.W.W.?

YANK. Naw. What is it?

VOICE. A gang of blokes – a tough gang. I been readin' about 'em today in the paper. The guard give me the 'Sunday Times'. There's a long spiel about 'em. It's from a speech made in the Senate by a guy named Senator Queen. (*He is in the cell next to YANK's. There is a rustling of paper.*) Wait'll I see if I got light enough and I'll read you. Listen. (*He reads.*) 'There is a menace existing in this country today which threatens the vitals of our fair Republic – as foul a menace against the very life-blood of the American Eagle as was the foul conspiracy of Cataline against the eagles of ancient Rome!'

VOICE (*disgustedly*). Aw hell! Tell him to salt de tail of dat eagle!

VOICE (*reading*). 'I refer to that devil's brew of rascals, jailbirds, murderers and cut-throats who libel all honest working-men by calling themselves the Industrial Workers of the World; but in the light of their nefarious plots, I call them the Industrious *Wreckers* of the World!'

YANK (*with vengeful satisfaction*). Wreckers dat's de right dope! Dat belongs! Me for dem!

VOICE. Ssshh! (*Reading.*) 'This fiendish organization is a foul ulcer on the fair body of our Democracy –'

VOICE. Democracy, hell! Give him the boid, fellers – the raspberry! (*They do.*)

VOICE. Ssshh! (*Reading*). 'Like Cato I say to this Senate, the I.W.W. must be destroyed! For they represent an ever-present dagger pointed at the heart of the greatest nation the world has ever known, where all men are born free and equal, with equal opportunities to all, where the Founding Fathers have guaranteed to each one happiness, where Truth, Honour, Liberty, Justice, and the Brotherhood of Man are a religion absorbed with one's mother's milk, taught at our father's knee, sealed, signed, and stamped upon in the glorious Constitution of these United States!' (*A perfect storm of hisses, catcalls, boos, and hard laughter.*)

VOICES (*scornfully*).
Hurrah for de Fort' of July!
Pass de hat!
Liberty!
Justice!
Honour!
Opportunity!
Brotherhood!

ALL (*with abysmal scorn*). Aw, hell!

VOICE. Give that Queen Senator guy the bark! All togedder now – one – two – tree – (*A terrific chorus of barking and yapping.*)

GUARD (*from a distance*). Quiet there, youse – or I'll git the hose. (*The noise subsides.*)

YANK (*with growling rage*). I'd like to catch dat senator guy alone for a second. I'd loin him some trute!

VOICE. Ssshh! Here's where he gits down to cases on the Wobblies. (*Reads.*) 'They plot with fire in one hand and dynamite in the other. They stop not before murder to gain their ends, nor at the outraging of defenceless womanhood. They would tear down society, put the lowest scum in the seats of the mighty, turn Almighty God's revealed plan for the world topsy-turvy, and make of our sweet and lovely civilization a shambles, a desolation, where man, God's masterpiece, would soon degenerate back to the ape!

VOICE (*to YANK.*) Hey, you guy! There's your ape stuff again.

YANK (*with a growl of fury*). I got him. So dey blow up tings, do dey? Dey turn tings round, do dey? Hey, lend me dat paper, will yuh?

VOICE. Sure. Give it to him. On'y keep it to yourself, see. We don't want listen to no more of that slop.

VOICE. Here you are. Hide it under your mattress.

YANK (*reaching out*). Tanks. I can't read much, but I kin manage. (*He sits, the paper in the hand at his side, in the attitude of Rodin's 'The Thinker'. A pause. Several snores from down the corridor. Suddenly* YANK *jumps to his feet with a furious groan as if some appalling thought had crashed on him.*) Sure – her old man – President of de Steel Trust – makes half de steel in de world – steel – where I tought I belonged – drivin' trou – movin' – in dat – to make *her* – and cage me in for her to spit on! Christ. (*He shakes the bars of his cell door till the whole tier trembles. Irritated, protesting exclamations from those awakened or trying to get to sleep.*) He made dis – dis cage! Steel! *It* don't belong, dat's what! Cages, cells, locks, bolts, bars – dat's what it means! – holdin' me down wit him at de top! But I'll drive trou! Fire, dat melts it! I'll be fire – under de heap – fire dat never goes out – hot as hell – breakin' out in de night –

While he has been saying this last he has shaken his cell door to a clanging accompaniment. As he comes to the 'breakin' out' he seizes one bar with both hands and, putting his two feet up against the others so that his position is parallel to the floor like a monkey's, he gives a great wrench backwards. The bar bends like a liquorice stick under his tremendous strength. Just at this moment the PRISON GUARD *rushes in, dragging a hose behind him.*

GUARD (*angrily*). I'll loin youse to wake me up! (*Sees* YANK.) Hallo, it's you, huh? Got the D.T.'s, hey? Well, I'll cure 'em. I'll drown your snakes for yuh! (*Noticing the bar*). Hell, look at dat bar bended! On'y a bug is strong enough for dat!

YANK (*glaring at him*). Or a hairy ape, yuh big yellow scut! Look out! Here I come! (*He grabs another bar.*)

GUARD (*scared now – yellowing off left*). Toin de hoose on, Ben! – full pressure! And call de others – and a strait-jacket! (*The curtain is falling. As it hides* YANK *from view, there is a splattering smash as the stream of water hits the steel of* YANK's *cell.*)

Curtain.

Scene Seven

*Scene. Nearly a month later. An I.W.W. local near the waterfront,
showing the interior of a front room on the ground-floor, and the street
outside. Moonlight on the narrow street, buildings massed in black
shadow. The interior of the room, which is general assembly room, office
and reading-room, resembles some dingy settlement boys' club. A desk and
high stool are in one corner. A table with paper, stacks of pamphlets,
chairs about it, is at centre. The whole is decidedly cheap, banal,
commonplace and unmysterious as a room could well be. The secretary is
perched on the stool making entries in a large ledger. An eye-shade casts
his face into shadows. Eight or ten men, longshoremen, iron workers, and
the like, are grouped about the table. Two are playing checkers. One is
writing a letter. Most of them are smoking pipes. A big signboard is on
the wall at the rear, 'Industrial Workers of the World – Local No. 57'.*

*YANK comes down the street outside. He is dressed at in Scene Five. He
moves cautiously, mysteriously. He comes to a point opposite the door;
tiptoes softly up to it, listens, is impressed by the silence within, knocks
carefully, as if he were guessing at the password to some secret rite.
Listens. No answer. Knocks again a bit louder. No answer. Knocks
impatiently, much louder.*

SECRETARY (*turning around on his stool*). What the devil is that –
some one knocking? (*Shouts.*) Come in, why don't you?

*All the men in the room look up. YANK opens the door slowly,
gingerly, as if afraid of an ambush. He looks around for secret doors,
mystery, is taken aback by the commonplaceness of the room and the
men in it, thinks he may have gotten in the wrong place, then sees the
signboard on the wall and is reassured.*

YANK (*blurts out*). Hallo!

MEN (*reservedly*). Hallo!

YANK (*more easily*). I tought I'd bumped into de wrong dump.

SECRETARY (*scrutinizing him carefully*). Maybe you have. Are you
a member?

YANK. Naw, not yet. Dat's what I come for – to join.

SECRETARY. That's easy. What's your job – longshore?

YANK. Naw. Fireman – stoker on de liners.

SECRETARY (*with satisfaction*). Welcome to our city. Glad to
know you people are waking up at last. We haven't got many
members in your line.

YANK. Naw. Dey're all dead to de woild.

SECRETARY. Well, you can help to wake 'em. What's your name? I'll make out a card.

YANK (*confused*). Name? Lemme tink.

SECRETARY (*sharply*). Don't you know your own name?

YANK. Sure; but I been just Yank for so long – Bob, dat's it – Bob Smith.

SECRETARY (*writing*). Robert Smith. (*Fills out the rest of card.*) Here you are. Cost you half a dollar.

YANK. Is dat all – four bits? Dat's easy. (*Gives the* SECRETARY *the money.*)

SECRETARY (*throwing it in drawer*). Thanks. Well, make yourself at home. No introductions needed. There's literature on the table. Take some of those pamphlets with you to distribute aboard ship. They may bring results. Sow the seed, only go about it right. Don't get caught and fired. We got plenty out of work. What we need is men who can hold their jobs – and work for us at the same time.

YANK. Sure. (*But he still stands, embarrassed and uneasy.*)

SECRETARY (*looking at him – curiously*). What did you knock for? Think we had a coon in uniform to open doors?

YANK. Naw. I tought it was locked – and dat yuh'd wanter give me the once-over trou a peep-hole or somep'n to see if I was right.

SECRETARY (*alert and suspicious, but with an easy laugh*). Think we were running a crap game? That door is never locked. What put that in your nut?

YANK (*with a knowing grin, convinced that this is all camouflage, a part of the secrecy*). Dis burg is full of bulls, ain't it?

SECRETARY (*sharply*). What have the cops got to do with us? We're breaking no laws.

YANK (*with a knowing wink*). Sure. Youse wouldn't for woilds. Sure. I'm wise to dat.

SECRETARY. You seem to be wise to a lot of stuff none of us knows about.

YANK (*with another wink*). Aw, dat's aw right, see. (*Then made a bit resentful by the suspicious glances from all sides.*) Aw, can it! Youse needn't put me trou de toid degree. Can't youse see I belong? Sure! I'm reg'lar. I'll stick, get me? I'll shoot de woiks for youse. Dat's why I wanted to join in.

SECRETARY (*breezily, feeling him out*). That's the right spirit. Only are you sure you understand what you've joined? It's all plain and above board; still some guys get a wrong slant on us. (*Sharply.*) What's your notion of the purpose of the I.W.W.?

YANK. Aw, I know all about it.

SECRETARY (*sarcastically*). Well, give us some of your valuable information.

YANK (*cunningly*). I know enough not to speak out-a my toin. (*Then resentfully again.*) Aw, say! I'm reg'lar. I'm wise to de game. I know yuh got to watch your step wit a stranger. For all youse know, I might be a plain-clothes dick, or somep'n, dat's what yuh're tinkin', huh? Aw, forget it! I belong, see? Ask any guy down to de docks if I don't.

SECRETARY. Who said you didn't?

YANK. After I'm 'nitiated, I'll show yuh.

SECRETARY (*astounded*). Initiated? There's no initiation.

YANK (*disappointed*). Ain't there no password – no grip nor nothin'?

SECRETARY. What'd you think this is – the Elks – or the Black Hand?

YANK. De Elks, hell! De Black Hand, dey're a lot of yellow backstickin' Ginees. Naw. Dis is a man's gang, ain't it?

SECRETARY. You said it! That's why we stand on our two feet in the open. We got no secrets.

YANK (*surprised but admiringly*). Yuh mean to say yuh always run wide open – like dis?

SECRETARY. Exactly.

YANK. Den yuh sure got your noive wit youse!

SECRETARY (*sharply*). Just what was it made you want to join us? Come out with that straight.

YANK. Yuh call me? Well, I got noive, too! Here's my hand. Yuh wanter blow tings up don't yuh? Well, dat's me! I belong!

SECRETARY (*with pretended carelessness*). You mean, change the unequal conditions of society by legitimate direct action – or with dynamite?

YANK. Dynamite! Blow it offen de oith – steel – all de cages – all de factories, steamers, buildings, jails – de Steel Trust and all dat makes it go.

SECRETARY. So – that's your idea, eh? And did you have any special job in that line you wanted to propose to us?

He makes a sign to the men, who get up cautiously one by one and group behind YANK.

YANK (*boldly*). Sure, I'll come out wit it. I'll show youse I'm one of de gang. Dere's dat millionaire guy, Douglas –

SECRETARY. President of the Steel Trust, you mean? Do you want to assassinate him?

YANK. Naw, dat don't get yuh nothin'. I mean blow up de factory, de woiks, where he makes de steel. Dat's what I'm after – to blow up de steel, knock all de steel in de woild up to de moon. Dat'll fix tings! (*Eagerly, with a touch of bravado.*) I'll do it by me lonesome! I'll show yuh! Tell me where his woiks is, how to git there, all de dope. Gimme de stuff, de old butter – and watch me do de rest! Watch de smoke and see it move! I don't give a damn if dey nab me – as long as it's done! I'll soive life for it – and give 'em de laugh! (*Half to himself.*) And I'll write her a letter and tell her de hairy ape done it. Dat'll square tings.

SECRETARY (*stepping away from YANK*). Very interesting.

He gives a signal. The men, huskies all, throw themselves on YANK, and before he knows it they have his legs and arms pinioned. But he is too flabbergasted to make a struggle, anyway. They feel him over for weapons.

MAN. No gat, no knife. Shall we give him what's what and put the boots to him?

SECRETARY. No. He isn't worth the trouble we'd get into. He's too stupid. (*He comes closer and laughs mockingly in YANK's face*). Ho-ho! By God, this is the biggest joke they've put up on us yet. Hey, you Joke! Who sent you – Burns or Pinkerton? No, by God, you're such a bonehead I'll bet you're in the Secret Service! Well, you dirty spy, you rotten agent provocateur, you can go back and tell whatever skunk is paying your blood-money for betraying your brothers that he's wasting his coin. You couldn't catch a cold. And tell him that all he'll ever get on us, or ever has got, is just his own sneaking plots that he's framed up to put us in jail. We are what our manifesto says we are, neither more nor less – and we'll give him a copy of that any time he calls. And as for you – (*He glares scornfully at* YANK, *who is sunk in an oblivious stupor.*) Oh, hell, what's the use of talking? You're a brainless ape.

YANK (*aroused by the word to fierce but futile struggles*). What's dat, yuh Sheeny, yuh!

SECRETARY. Throw him out, boys.

In spite of his struggles, this is done with gusto and éclat. Propelled by several parting kicks, YANK *lands sprawling in the middle of the narrow cobbled street. With a growl he starts to get up and storm the closed door, but stops bewildered by the confusion in his brain, pathetically impotent. He sits there, brooding, in as near to the attitude of Rodin's 'Thinker' as he can get in his position.*

YANK (*bitterly*). So dem boids don't tink I belong, neider. Aw, to hell wit 'em! Dey're in de wrong pew – de same old bull – soapboxes and Salvation Army – no guts! Cut out an hour offen de job a day and make me happy! Gimme a dollar more a day and make me happy! Tree square a day, and cauliflowers in de front yard – ekal rights – a woman and kids – a lousey vote – and I'm all fixed for Jesus, huh? Aw, hell! What does dat get yuh? Dis ting's in your inside, but it ain't in your belly. Feedin' your face – sinkers and coffee – dat don't touch it. It's way down – at de bottom. Yuh can't grab it, and yuh can't stop it. It moves, and everyting moves. It stops and de whole woild stops. Dat's me now – I don't tick, see? – I'm a busted Ingersoll, dat's what. Steel was me, and I owned de woild. Now I ain't steel, and de woild owns me. Aw, hell! I can't see – it's all dark, get me? It's all wrong! (*He turns a bitter, mocking face up like an ape gibbering at the moon.*) Say, youse up dere, Man in de Moon, yuh look so wise, gimme de answer, huh? Slip me de inside dope, de information right from de stable – where do I get off at, huh?

A POLICEMAN (*who has come up the street in time to hear this last – with grim humour*). You'll get off at the station, you boob, if you don't get up out of that and keep movin'.

YANK (*looking up at him – with a hard, bitter laugh.*) Sure! Lock me up! Put me in a cage! Dat's de on'y answer yuh know. G'wan, lock me up!

POLICEMAN. What you been doin'?

YANK. Enuf to gimme life for! I was born, see? Sure, dat's de charge. Write it in de blotter. I was born, get me!

POLICEMAN (*jocosely*). God pity your old woman! (*Then matter-of-fact.*) But I've no time for kidding. You're soused. I'd run you in but it's too long a walk to the station. Come on now, get up, or I'll fan your ears with this club. Beat it now! (*He hauls YANK to his feet.*)

YANK (*in a vague, mocking tone*). Say, where do I go from here?

POLICEMAN (*giving him a push – with a grin indifferently*). Go to hell.
  Curtain.

Scene Eight

Scene. Twilight of the next day. The monkey-house at the Zoo. One spot of clear, grey light falls on the front of one cage so that the interior can be seen. The other cages are vague, shrouded in shadow from which chatterings pitched in a conversational tone can be heard. On the one cage a sign from which the word 'gorilla' stands out. The gigantic animal himself is seen squatting on his haunches on a bench in much the same attitude as Rodin's 'Thinker'. YANK enters from the left. Immediately a chorus of angry chattering and screeching breaks out. The gorilla turns his eyes, but makes no sound or move.

YANK (*with a hard, bitter laugh*). Welcome to your city, huh? Hail, hail, de gang's all here! (*At the sound of his voice the chattering dies away into an attentive silence. YANK walks up to the gorilla's cage and, leaning over the railing, stares in at its occupant, who stares back at him, silent and motionless. There is a pause of dead stillness. Then YANK begins to talk in a friendly, confidential tone, half-mockingly, but with a deep undercurrent of sympathy.*) Say, yuh're some hard-lookin' guy, ain't yuh? I seen lots of tough nuts dat de gang called gorillas, but yuh're de foist real one I ever seen. Some chest yuh got, and shoulders, and dem arms and mits! I bet yuh got a punch in eider fist dat'd knock 'em silly! (*This with genuine admiration. The gorilla, as if he understood, stands upright, swelling out his chest and pounding on it with his fist. YANK grins sympathetically.*) Sure, I get yuh. Yuh challenge de whole woild, huh? Yuh got what I was sayin' even if yuh muffed de woids. (*Then bitterness creeping in.*) And why wouldn't yuh get me? Ain't we both members of de same club – de Hairy Apes? (*They stare*

at each other – a pause – then YANK *goes on slowly and bitterly.*) So
yuh're what she seen when she looked at me, de white-faced
tart! I was you to her, get me? On'y outa de cage – broke out –
free to moider her, see? Sure! Dat's what she tought. She wasn't
wise dat I was in a cage, too – worser'n yours – sure – a damn
sight – 'cause you got some chanct to bust loose – but me – (*He
grows confused.*) Aw hell! It's all wrong, ain't it? (*A pause.*) I
s'pose yuh wanter know what I'm doin' here, huh? I been
warmin' a bench down to de Battery – ever since last night.
Sure. I seen de sun come up. Dat was pretty, too – all red and
pink and green. I was lookin' at de skyscrapers – steel – and all
de ships comin' in, sailin' out, all over de oith – and dey was
steel, too. De sun was warm, dey wasn't no clouds, and dere
was a breeze blowin'. Sure, it was great stuff. I got it aw right –
what Paddy said about dat bein' de right dope – on'y I couldn't
get *in* it, see? I couldn't belong in dat. It was over my head.
And I kept tinkin' – and den I beat it up here to see what
youse was like. And I waited till dey was all gone to git yuh
alone. Say, how d'yuh feel sittin' in dat pen all de time, havin'
to stand for 'em comin' and starin' at yuh – de white-faced,
skinny tarts and de boobs what marry 'em – makin' fun of yuh,
laughin' at yuh, gittin' scared of yuh – damn 'em! (*He pounds on
the rail with his fist. The gorilla rattles the bars of his cage and snarls.
All the other monkeys set up an angry chattering in the darkness.
YANK goes on excitedly.*) Sure! Dat's de way it hits me, too. On'y
yuh're lucky, see? Yuh don't belong wit 'em and yuh know it.
But me, I belong wit 'em – but I don't, see? Dey don't belong wit
me, dat's what. Get me? Tinkin' is hard – (*He passes one hand across
his forehead with a painful gesture. The gorilla growls impatiently.
YANK goes on gropingly.*) It's dis way, what I'm drivin' at. Youse
can sit and dope dream in de past, green woods, de jungle and
de rest of it. Den yuh belong and dey don't. Den yuh kin laugh
at 'em see? Yuh're de champ of de woild. But me – I ain't got
no past to tink in, nor nothin' dat's comin', on'y what's now –
and dat don't belong. Sure, you're de best off! Yuh can't tink,
can yuh? Yuh can't talk neider. But I kin make a bluff at talkin'
and tinkin' – a'most git away wit it – a'most! – and dat's where
de joker comes in. (*He laughs.*) I ain't on oith and I ain't in
Heaven, get me? I'm in de middle tryin' to separate 'em, takin'
all de woist punches from bot' of 'em. Maybe dat's what dey call
Hell, uh? But you, yuh're at de bottom. You belong! Sure!
Yuh're de on'y one in de woild dat does, yuh lucky stiff! (*The
gorilla growls proudly.*) And dat's why dey gotter put yuh in a
cage, see? (*The gorilla roars angrily.*) Sure! Yuh get me. It beats it

when you try to tink it or talk it – it's way down – deep –
behind – you'n me we feel it. Sure! Bot' members of dis club!
(*He laughs – then in a savage tone.*) What de hell! T' hell wit it! A
little action, dat's our meat! Dat belongs! Knock em down and
keep bustin' 'em till dey croaks yuh wit a gat – wit steel! Sure!
Are yuh game? Dey've looked at youse, ain't dey – in a cage?
Wanter git even? Wanter wind up like a sport 'stead of croakin'
slow in dere? (*The gorilla roars an emphatic affirmative.* YANK
goes on with a sort of furious exaltation.) Sure! Yuh're reg'lar!
Yuh'll stick to de finish! Me'n you, huh? – bot' members of this
club! We'll put up one last star bout dat'll knock 'em offen deir
seats! Dey'll have to make de cages stronger after we're trou!
(*The gorilla is straining at his bars, growling, hopping from one foot to
the other.* YANK *takes a jimmy from under his coat and forces the lock
on the cage door. He throws this open*). Pardon from de governor!
Step out and shake hands! I'll take yuh for a walk down Fif'
Avenoo. We'll knock 'em offen de oith and croak wit de band
playin'. Come on, Brother. (*The gorilla scrambles gingerly out of his
cage. Goes to* YANK *and stands looking at him.* YANK *keeps his
mocking tone – holds out his hand.*) Shake – de secret grip of our
order. (*Something, the tone of mockery, perhaps, suddenly enrages the
animal. With a spring he wraps his huge arms around* YANK *in a
murderous hug. There is a crackling snap of crushed ribs – a gasping
cry, still mocking, from* YANK.) Hey, I didn't say kiss me. (*The
gorilla lets the crushed body slip to the floor; stands over it uncertainly,
considering; then picks it up, throws it in the cage, shuts the door, and
shuffles off menacingly into the darkness at left. A great uproar of
frightened chattering and whimpering comes from the other cages. Then*
YANK *moves, groaning, opening his eyes, and there is silence. He
mutters painfully.*) Say – dey oughter match him – wit Zybszko.
He got me, aw right. I'm trou. Even him didn't tink I belonged.
(*Then, with sudden, passionate despair.*) Christ, where do I get off?
Where do I fit in? (*Checking himself as suddenly.*) Aw, what de
hell! No squakin', see! No quittin', get me! Croak wit your boots
on! (*He grabs hold of the bars of the cage and hauls himself painfully
to his feet – looks around him, bewildered – forces a mocking laugh.*)
In de cage huh? (*In the strident tones of a circus barker.*) Ladies
and gents, step forward and take a slant at de one and only –
(*his voice weakening*) – one and original – Hairy Ape from de
wilds of – (*He slips in a heap on the floor and dies. The monkeys set
up a chattering, whimpering wail. And, perhaps, the Hairy Ape at last
belongs.*

Curtain.

ALL GOD'S CHILLUN GOT WINGS

Characters

JIM HARRIS
MRS HARRIS, his mother
HATTIE, his sister
ELLA DOWNEY
SHORTY
JOE
MICKEY
WHITES AND NEGROES

Scenes

ACT ONE

Scene One. A corner in lower New York. Years ago. End of an afternoon in spring.

Scene Two. The same. Nine years later. End of an evening in spring.

Scene Three. The same. Five years later. A night in spring.

Scene Four. The street before a church in the same ward. A morning some weeks later.

ACT TWO

Scene One. A flat in the same ward. A morning two years later.

Scene Two. The same. At twilight some months later.

Scene Three. The same. A night some months later.

ACT ONE

Scene One

Scene. A corner in lower New York, at the edge of a coloured district. Three narrow streets converge. A triangular building in the rear, red brick, four-storied, its ground floor a grocery. Four-storey tenements stretch away down the skyline of the two streets. The fire escapes are crowded with people. In the street leading left, the faces are all white; in the street leading right, all black. It is hot Spring. On the sidewalk are eight children, four boys and four girls. Two of each sex are white, two black. They are playing marbles. One of the black boys is JIM HARRIS. *The little blonde girl, her complexion rose and white, who sits behind his elbow and holds his marbles is* ELLA DOWNEY. *She is eight. They play the game with concentrated attention for a while. People pass, black and white, the Negroes frankly participants in the spirit of Spring, the whites laughing constrainedly, awkward in natural emotion. Their words are lost. One only hears their laughter. It expresses the difference in race. There are street noises – the clattering roar of the Elevated, the puff of its locomotives, the ruminative lazy sound of a horse-car, the hoofs of its team clacking on the cobbles From the street of the whites a high-pitched, nasal tenor sings the chorus of 'Only a Bird in a Gilded Cage.' On the street of the blacks a Negro strikes up the chorus of: 'I Guess I'll Have to Telegraph My Baby.' As this singing ends, there is laughter, distinctive in quality, from both streets. Then silence. The light in the street begins to grow brilliant with the glow of the setting sun. The game of marbles goes on.*

WHITE GIRL (*tugging at the elbow of her brother*). Come on, Mickey!

HER BROTHER (*roughly*). Aw, gwan, youse!

WHITE GIRL. Aw right den. You kingit a lickin' if you wanter. (*Gets up to move off.*)

HER BROTHER. Aw, git off de eart'!

WHITE GIRL. De old woman'll be madder'n hell!

HER BROTHER (*worried now*). I'm comin', ain't I! Hold your horses.

BLACK GIRL (*to a black boy*). Come on, you Joe. We gwine git frailed too, you don't hurry.

JOE. Go long!

MICKEY. Bust up de game, huh? I gotta run! (*Jumps to his feet.*)

OTHER WHITE BOY. Me, too! (*Jumps up.*)

OTHER BLACK GIRL. Lawdy, it's late!

JOE. Me for grub!

MICKEY (*to* JIM HARRIS.) You's de winner, Jim Crow. Yeh gotta play tomorrer.

JIM (*readily*). Sure t'ing, Mick. Come one, come all! (*He laughs.*)

OTHER WHITE BOY. Me too! I gotta git back at yuh.

JIM. Aw right, Shorty.

LITTLE GIRLS. Hurry! Come on, come on!

The six start off together. Then they notice that JIM *and* ELLA *are hesitating, standing awkwardly and shyly together. They turn to mock.*

JOE. Look at dat Jim Crow! Land sakes, he got a gal! (*He laughs. They all laugh.*)

JIM (*ashamed*). Ne're mind, you Chocolate!

MICKEY. Look ta de two softies, will yeh! Mush! Mush! (*He and the two other boys take this up.*)

LITTLE GIRLS (*pointing their fingers at* ELLA). Shame! Shame! Everybody knows your name! Painty Face! Painty Face!

ELLA (*hanging her head*). Shut up!

LITTLE WHITE GIRL. He's been carrying her books!

COLOURED GIRL. Can't you find nuffin' better'n him, Ella? Look at de big feet he got! (*She laughs. They all laugh.* JIM *puts one foot on top of the other, looking at* ELLA.)

ELLA. Mind yer own business, see! (*She strides towards them angrily. They jump up and dance in an ecstasy, screaming and laughing.*)

ALL. Found yeh out! Found yeh out!

MICKEY. Mush-head! Jim Crow de Sissy! Stuck on Painty Face!

JOE. Will Painty Face let you hold her doll, boy?

SHORTY. Sissy! Softy! (ELLA *suddenly begins to cry. At this they all howl.*)

ALL. Cry-baby! Cry-baby! Look at her! Painty Face!

JIM (*suddenly rushing them, with clenched fists, furiously*). Shut yo' moufs! I kin lick de hull of you! (*They all run away, laughing, shouting, and jeering, quite triumphant now that they have made him, too, lose his temper. He comes back to* ELLA, *and stands beside her sheepishly, stepping on one foot after the other. Suddenly he blurts out:*) Don't bawl no more. I done chased 'em.

ELLA (*comforted, politely*). T'anks.

JIM (*swelling out*). It was a cinch. I kin wipe up de street wid any one of dem. (*He stretches out his arms, trying to bulge out his biceps.*) Feel dat muscle!

ELLA (*does so gingerly – then with admiration*). My!

JIM (*protectingly*). You mustn't never be scared when I'm hanging round, Painty Face.

ELLA. Don't call me that, Jim – please!

JIM (*contritely*). I didn't mean nuffin', I didn't know you'd mind.

ELLA. I do – more'n anything.

JIM. You oughtn't to mind. Dey's jealous, dat's what.

ELLA. Jealous? Of what?

JIM (*pointing to her face*). Of dat. Red 'n' white. It's purty.

ELLA. I hate it!

JIM. It's purty. Yes, it's – it's purty. It's – outa sight!

ELLA. I hate it. I wish I was black like you.

JIM (*sort of shrinking*). No, you don't. Dey'd call you Crow, den – or Chocolate – or Smoke.

ELLA. I wouldn't mind.

JIM (*sombrely*). Dey'd call you nigger sometimes, too.

ELLA. I wouldn't mind.

JIM (*humbly*). You wouldn't mind?

ELLA. No, I wouldn't mind. (*An awkward pause.*)

JIM (*suddenly*). You know what, Ella? Since I been tuckin' yo' books to school and back, I been drinkin' lots o' chalk 'n' water three times a day. Dat Tom, de barber, he tole me dat make me white, if I drink enough. (*Pleadingly.*) Does I look whiter?

ELLA (*comfortingly*). Yes – maybe – a little bit –

JIM (*trying a careless tone*). Reckon dat Tom's a liar, an' de joke's on me! Dat chalk only makes me feel kinder sick inside.

ELLA (*wonderingly*). Why do you want to be white?

JIM. Because – just because – I lak dat better.

ELLA. I wouldn't. I like black. Let's you and me swap. I'd like to be black. (*Clapping her hands.*) Gee, that'd be fun, if we only could!

JIM (*hesitantly*). Yes – maybe –

ELLA. Then they'd call me Crow, and you'd be Painty Face!

JIM. They wouldn't never dast call you nigger, you bet! I'd kill 'em! (*A long pause. Finally she takes his hand shyly. They both keep looking as far away from each other as possible*).

ELLA. I like you.

JIM. I like you.

ELLA. Do you want to be my feller?

JIM. Yes.

ELLA. Then I'm your girl.

JIM. Yes. (*Then grandly.*) You kin bet none o' de gang gwine call you Painty Face from dis out! I lam' 'em good! (*The sun has set. Twilight has fallen on the street. An organgrinder comes up to the corner and plays 'Annie Rooney.' They stand hand-in-hand and listen. He goes away. It is growing dark.*)

ELLA (*suddenly*). Golly it's late! I'll git a lickin'!

JIM. Me, too.

ELLA. I won't mind it much.

JIM. Me nuther.

ELLA. See you going to school tomorrow?

JIM. Sure.

ELLA. I gotta skip now.

JIM. Me, too.

ELLA. I like you, Jim.

JIM. I like you.

ELLA. Don't forget.

JIM. Don't you.

ELLA. Goodbye.

JIM. So long. (*They run away from each other – then stop abruptly, and turn as at a signal.*)

ELLA. Don't forget.

JIM. I won't, you bet!

ELLA. Here! (*She kisses her hand at him, then runs off in frantic embarrassment.*)

JIM (*overcome*). Gee!

Then he turns and darts away, as the curtain falls.

Scene Two

Scene. The same corner. Nine years have passed. It is again late Spring at a time in the evening which immediately follows the hour of Scene One. Nothing has changed much. One street is still all white, the other all black. The fire escapes are laden with drooping human beings. The grocery store is still at the corner. The street noises are now more rhythmically mechanical, electricity having taken the place of horse and steam. People pass, white and black. They laugh as in Scene One. From the street of the whites the high-pitched nasal tenor sings, 'Gee, I Wish That I Had a Girl,' and the Negro replies with, 'All I Got Was Sympathy.' The singing is followed again by laughter from both streets. Then silence. The dusk grows darker. With a spluttering flare the arc-lamp at the corner is lit and sheds a pale glare over the street. Two young roughs slouch up to the corner, as tough in manner as they can make themselves. One is the SHORTY *of Scene One; the other the Negro* JOE. *They stand loafing. A boy of seventeen or so passes by, escorting a girl of about the same age. Both are dressed in their best, the boy in black with stiff collar, the girl in white.*

SHORTY (*scornfully*). Hully cripes! Pipe who's here. (*To the girl, sneeringly.*) Wha's matter, Liz. Don't yer recernize yer old fr'en's?

GIRL (*frightenedly*). Hello, Shorty.

SHORTY. Why de glad rags? Goin' to graduation? (*He tries to obstruct their way, but, edging away from him, they turn and run.*)

JOE. Har-har! Look at dem scoot, will you! (SHORTY *grins with satisfaction.*)

SHORTY (*looking down other street*). Here comes Mickey.

JOE. He won de semi-final last night easy?

SHORTY. Knocked de bloke out in de thoid.

JOE. Dat boy's suah a-comin! He'll be de champeen yit.

SHORTY (*judicially*). Got a good chanct – if he leaves de broads alone. Dat's where he's wide open.

MICKEY *comes in from the left. He is dressed loudly, a straw hat with a gaudy band cocked over one cauliflower ear. He has acquired a typical 'pug's' face, with the added viciousness of a natural bully. 'one of his eyes is puffed, almost closed, as a result of his battle the night before. He swaggers up.*

BOTH. Hello, Mickey!

MICKEY. Hello!

JOE. Hear you knocked him col'.

MICKEY. Sure. I knocked his block off. (*Changing the subject.*) Say. Seen 'em goin' past to de graduation racket?

SHORTY (*with a wink*). Why? You int'rested?

JOE (*chuckling*). Mickey's gwine roun' git a good conduct medal.

MICKEY. Sure. Dey kin pin it on de seat o' me pants. (*They laugh.*) Listen. Seen Ella Downey goin'?

SHORTY. Painty Face? No, she ain' been along.

MICKEY (*with authority*). Can dat name, see! Want a bunch o' fives in her kisser? Den nix! She's me goil, understan'?

JOE (*venturing to joke*). Which one? Yo' number ten?

MICKEY (*flattered*). Sure. De real K.O. one.

SHORTY (*pointing right – sneeringly*). Gee! Pipe Jim Crow all dolled up for de racket.

JOE (*with disgusted resentment*). You mean tell me dat nigger's graduatin'?

SHORTY. Ask him. (JIM HARRIS *comes in. He is dressed in black, stiff white collar, etc. – a quiet-mannered Negro boy with a queerly-baffled, sensitive face.*)

JIM (*pleasantly*). Hello, fellows! (*They grunt in reply, looking over him scornfully.*)

JOE (*staring resentfully*). Is you graduatin' tonight?

JIM. Yes.

JOE (*spitting disgustedly*). For Gawd's sake! You *is* gittin' high-falutin'!

JIM (*smiling deprecatingly*). This is my second try. I didn't pass last year.

JOE. What de hell does it gat you, huh? Whatever is you gwine do wid it now you gits it? Live lazy on yo' ol' woman?

JIM (*assertively*). I'm going to study and become a lawyer.

JOE (*with a snort*). Fo' Chris' sake, nigger!

JIM (*fiercely*). Don't you call me that – not before them!

JOE (*pugnaciously*). Does you deny you's a nigger? I shows you –

MICKEY (*gives them both a push – truculently*). Cut it out, see! I'm runnin' dis corner. (*Turning to* JIM *insultingly.*) Say, you! Painty Face's gittin' her ticket tonight ain't she?

JIM. You mean Ella –

MICKEY. Painty Face Downey, dat's who I mean! I don't have to be perlite wit' her. She's me goil!

JIM (*glumly*). Yes, she's graduating.

SHORTY (*winks at* MICKEY). Smart, huh?

MICKEY (*winks back – meaningly*). Willin' to loin, take it from me! (*JIM stands tensely as if a struggle were going on in him.*)

JIM (*finally blurts out*). I want to speak to you Mickey – alone.

MICKEY (*surprised – insultingly*). Aw, what de hell – !

JIM (*excitedly*). It's important, I tell you!

MICKEY. Huh? (*Stares at him inquisitively – then motions the others back carelessly and follows* JIM *down front.*)

SHORTY. Some noive!

JOE (*vengefully*). I gits dat Jim alone, you wait!

MICKEY. Well, spill de big news. I ain't got all night. I got a date.

JIM. With – Ella?

MICKEY. What's dat to you?

JIM (*the words tumbling out*). What – I wanted to say! – I know – I've heard – all the stories – what you've been doing around the ward – with other girls – it's none of my business, with them – but she – Ella – it's different – she's not that kind –

MICKEY (*insultingly*). Who told yuh so, huh?

JIM (*draws back his fist threateningly*). Don't you dare – ! (MICKEY *is so paralysed by this effrontery that he actually steps back.*)

MICKEY. Say, cut de comedy! (*Beginning to feel insulted.*) Listen you Jim Crow! Ain't you wise I could give yuh one poke dat'd knock yuh into next week?

JIM. I'm only asking you to act square, Mickey.

MICKEY. What's it to yuh? Why, yuh lousey goat, she wouldn't spit on yuh even! She hates de sight of a coon.

JIM (*in agony*). I – I know – but once she didn't mind – we were kids together –

MICKEY. Aw, ferget dat! Dis is *now*!

JIM. And I'm still her friend always – even if she don't like coloured people –

MICKEY. *Coons*, why don't yuh say it right! De trouble wit' yoh is yuh're gittin' stuck up, dat's what! Stay where yeh belong, see! Yer old man made coin at de truckin' game and yuh're tryin' to buy yerself white – graduatin' and law, for hell's sake! Yuh're gittin' yerself in Dutch wit' everyone in de ward – and it ain't cause yer a coon neider. Don't be gang all train wit' Joe dere and lots of others? But yuh're tryin' to buy white and it won't git yuh no place, see!

JIM (*trembling*). Some day – I'll show you –

MICKEY (*turning away*). Aw, gwan!

JIM. D'you think I'd change – be you – your dirty white –

MICKEY (*whirling about*). What'd dat?

JIM (*with hysterical vehemence*). You act square with her – or I'll show you up – I'll report you – I'll write to the papers – the sporting writers – I'll let them know how white you are!

MICKEY (*infuriated*). Yuh damn nigger, I'll bust yer jaw in!

(*Assuming his ring pose he weaves toward* JIM, *his face set in a cruel scowl.* JIM *waits helplessly but with a certain dignity.*)

SHORTY. Cheese it! A couple bulls! And here's de Downey skoit comin', too.

MICKEY. I'll get yuh de next time!

ELLA DOWNEY *enters from the right. She is seventeen, still has the same rose-and-white complexion, is pretty but with a rather repelling bold air about her.*

ELLA (*smiles with pleasure when she sees* MICKEY. Hello, Mick! Am I late? Say, I'm so glad you won last night. (*She glances from one to the other as she feels something in the air.*) Hello! What's up?

MICKEY. Dis boob. (*He indicates* JIM *scornfully.*)

JIM (*diffidently*). Hello, Ella!

ELLA (*shortly, turning away*). Hello! (*Then to* MICKEY.) Come on, Mick. Walk down with me. I got to hurry.

JIM (*blurts out*). Wait – just a second. (*Painfully.*) Ella, do you hate – coloured people?

MICKEY. Aw, shut up!

JIM. Please answer.

ELLA (*forcing a laugh*). Say! What is this – another exam?

JIM (*doggedly*). Please answer.

ELLA (*irritably*). Of course I don't! Haven't I been brought up alongside – Why, some of my oldest – the girls I've been to public school the longest with –

JIM. Do you hate me, Ella?

ELLA (*confusedly and more irritably*). Say, is he drunk? Why should I? I don't hate anyone.

JIM. Then why haven't you ever hardly spoken to me – for years?

ELLA (*resentfully*). What would I speak about? You and me've got nothing in common any more.

JIM (*desperately*). Maybe not any more – but – right on this corner – do you remember once – ?

ELLA. I don't remember nothing! (*Angrily.*) Say! What's got into you to be butting into my business all of a sudden like this?

Because you finally managed to graduate, has it gone to your head?

JIM. No, I – only want to help you, Ella.

ELLA. Of all the nerve! You're certainly forgetting your place! Who's asking you for help, I'd like to know? Shut up and stop bothering me!

JIM (*insistently*). If you ever need a friend – a true friend –

ELLA. I've got lots of friends among my own – kind, I can tell you. (*Exasperatedly.*) You make me sick! Go to – hell! (*She flounces off. The three men laugh. MICKEY follows her. JIM is stricken. He goes and sinks down limply on a box in front of the grocery store.*)

SHORTY. I'm going to shoot a drink. Come on, Joe, and I'll blow yuh.

JOE (*who has never ceased to follow every move of JIM's with angry, resentful eyes.*) Go long. I'se gwine stay here a secon'. I got a lil' argyment. (*He points to JIM.*)

SHORTY. Suit yerself. Do a good job. See yuh later. (*He goes, whistling.*)

JOE (*stands for a while glaring at JIM, his fierce little eyes peering out of his black face. Then he spits on his hands aggressively and strides up to the oblivious JIM. He stands in front of him, gradually working himself into a fury at the other's seeming indifference to his words.*) Listen to me, nigger: I got a heap to whisper in yo' ear! Who is you, anyhow? Who does you think you is? Don't yo' old man and mine work on de docks togidder befo' yo' old man gits his own truckin' business? Yo' ol' man swallers his nickels, my ol' man buys him beer wid dem and swallers dat – dat's the on'y diff'rence. Don't you 'n' me drag up togidder?

JIM (*dully*). I'm your friend, Joe.

JOE. No, you isn't! I ain't no fren' o' yourn! I don't even know who you is! What's all dis schoolin' you doin'? What's all dis dressin' up and graduatin' an' sayin' you gwine study be a lawyer? What's all dis fakin' an' pretendin' and swellin' out grand an' talkin' soft and perlite? What's all dis denyin' you's a nigger – an' wid de white boys listenin' to you say it! Is you aimin' to buy white wid yo' ol' man's dough like Mickey say? What is you? (*In a rage at the other's silence.*) You don't talk? Den I takes it out o' yo' hide! (*He grabs JIM by the throat with one hand and draws the other fist back.*) Tell me befo' I wrecks yo' face in!

Is you a nigger or isn't you? (*Shaking him.*) Is you a nigger, Nigger? Nigger, is you a nigger?

JIM (*looking into his eyes – quietly*). Yes. I'm a nigger. We're both niggers. (*They look at each other for a moment. JOE's rage vanishes. He slumps on to a box beside JIM's. He offers him a cigarette. JIM takes it. JOE scratches a match and lights both their cigarettes.*)

JOE (*after a puff, with full satisfaction*). Man, why didn't you 'splain dat in de fust place?

JIM. We're both niggers. (*The same hand-organ man of Scene One comes to the corner. He plays the chorus of 'Bonbon Buddie', the 'Chocolate Drop'. They both stare straight ahead listening. Then the organ man goes away. A silence. JOE gets to his feet.*)

JOE. I'll go get me a cold beer. (*He starts to move off – then turns.*) Time you was graduatin', ain't it?

He goes, JIM remains sitting on his box staring straight before him as the curtain falls.

Scene Three

Scene. The same corner five years later. Nothing has changed much. It is a night in Spring. The arc-lamp discovers faces with a favourless cruelty. The street noises are the same but more intermittent and dulled with a quality of fatigue. Two people pass, one black and one white. They are tired. They both yawn, but neither laughs. There is no laughter from the two streets. From the street of the whites the tenor, more nasal than ever and a bit drunken, wails in high barber-shop falsetto the last half of the chorus of 'When I Lost You'. The Negro voice, a bit maudlin in turn, replies with the last half of 'Waiting for the Robert E. Lee.' Silence. SHORTY enters. He looks tougher than ever, the typical gangster. He stands waiting, singing a bit drunkenly, peering down the street.

SHORTY (*indignantly*). Yuh bum! Ain't yuh ever comin'? (*He begins to sing: 'And sewed up in her yeller kimona, She had a blue-barrelled forty-five gun, For to get her man Who'd done her wrong.' Then he comments scornfully.*) Not her, dough! No gat for her. She ain't got de noive. A little sugar. Dat'll fix her.

ELLA enters. She is dressed poorly, her face is pale and hollow-eyed, her voice cold and tired.

SHORTY. Yuh got de message?

ELLA. Here I am.

SHORTY. How yuh been?

ELLA. All right. (*A pause. He looks at her puzzledly.*)

SHORTY (*a bit embarrassedly*). Well, I s'pose yuh'd like me to give yuh some dope on Mickey, huh?

ELLA. No.

SHORTY. Mean to say yuh don't wanter know where he is or what he's doin?

ELLA. No.

SHORTY. Since when?

ELLA. A long time.

SHORTY (*after a pause – with a rat-like viciousness*). Between you'n me, kid, you'll get even soon – you'n all de odder dames he's tossed. I'm on de inside. I've watched him trainin'. His next scrap, watch it! He'll go! It won't be de odder guy. It'll be all youse dames he's kidded – and de ones what's kidded him. Youse'll all be in de odder guy's corner. He won't need no odder seconds. Youse'll trow water on him, and sponge his face, and take de kinks out of his socker – and Mickey'll catch it on de button – and he won't be able to take it no more – 'cause all your weight – you and de odders – 'll be behind dat punch. Ha, ha! (*He laughs an evil laugh.*) And Mickey'll go – down to his knees first – (*He sinks to his knees in the attitude of a groggy boxer.*)

ELLA. I'd like to see him on his knees!

SHORTY. And den – flat on his pan – dead to de world – de boidies singin' in de trees – ten – out! (*He suits his action to the words, sinking flat on the pavement, then rises and laughs the same evil laugh.*)

ELLA. He's been out – for me – a long time. (*A pause.*) Why did you send for me?

SHORTY. He sent me.

ELLA. Why?

SHORTY. To slip you this wad o' dough. (*He reluctantly takes a roll of bills from his pocket and hoids it out to her.*)

ELLA (*looks at the money indifferently*). What for?

SHORTY. For you.

ELLA. No.

SHORTY. For de kid den.

ELLA. The kid's dead. He took diphtheria.

SHORTY. Hell yuh say! When?

ELLA. A long time.

SHORTY. Why didn't you write Mickey – ?

ELLA. Why should I? He'd only be glad.

SHORTY (*after a pause*). Well – it's better.

ELLA. Yes.

SHORTY. You made up wit yer family?

ELLA. No chance.

SHORTY. Livin' alone?

ELLA. In Brooklyn.

SHORTY. Workin'?

ELLA. In a factory.

SHORTY. You're a sucker. There's lots of softer snaps for you, kid –

ELLA. I know what you mean. No.

SHORTY. Don't yuh wanter step out no more – have fun – live?

ELLA. I'm through.

SHORTY (*mockingly*). Jump in de river, huh? T'ink it over, baby. I kin start yuh right in my stable. No one'll bodder yuh den. I got influence.

ELLA (*without emphasis*). You're a dirty dog. Why doesn't someone kill you?

SHORTY. Is dat so! What're you? They say you been travellin' round with Jim Crow.

ELLA. He's been my only friend.

SHORTY. A nigger!

ELLA. The only white man in the world! Kind and white. You're all black – black to the heart.

SHORTY. Nigger-lover! (*He throws the money in her face. It falls to the street.*) Listen, you! Mickey says he's off of yuh for keeps. Dis is de finish! Dat's what he sent me to tell you. (*Glances at her searchingly – a pause.*) Yuh won't make no trouble?

ELLA. Why should I? He's free. The kid's dead. I'm free. No hard feelings – only – I'll be there in spirit at his next fight, tell him! I'll take your tip – the other corner – second the punch – nine – ten – out! He's free! That's all. (*She grins horribly at* SHORTY.) Go away, Shorty.

SHORTY (*looking at her and shaking his head – maudlinly*). Groggy! Groggy! We're all groggy! Gluttons for punishment! Me for a drink. So long.

He goes. A Salvation Army band comes toward the corner. They are playing and singing 'Till We Meet at Jesus' Feet.' They reach the end as they enter and stop before ELLA. *The* CAPTAIN *steps forward.*

CAPTAIN. Sister –

ELLA (*picks up the money and drops it in his hat – mockingly*). Here. Go save yourself. Leave me alone.

A WOMAN SALVATIONIST. Sister –

ELLA. Never mind that. I'm not in your line – yet. (*As they hesitate, wonderingly.*) I want to be alone.

To the thud of the big drum they march off. ELLA *sits down on a box, her hands hanging at her sides. Presently* JIM HARRIS *comes in. He has grown into a quietly-dressed, studious-looking Negro with an intelligent yet queerly-baffled face.*

JIM (*with a joyous but bewildered cry*). Ella! I just saw Shorty –

ELLA (*smiling at him with frank affection*). He had a message from Mickey.

JIM (*sadly*). Ah!

ELLA (*pointing to the box behind her*). Sit down. (*He does so. A pause – then she says indifferently.*) It's finished. I'm free, Jim.

JIM (*wearily*). We're never free – except to do what we have to do.

ELLA. What are you getting gloomy about all of a sudden?

JIM. I've got the report from the school. I've flunked again.

ELLA. Poor Jim!

JIM. Don't pity me. I'd like to kick myself all over the block. Five years – and I'm still plugging away where I ought to have been at the end of two.

ELLA. Why don't you give it up?

JIM. No!

ELLA. After all, what's being a lawyer?

JIM. A lot – to me – what it means. (*Intensely.*) Why, if I was a Member of the bar right now, Ella, I believe I'd almost have the courage to –

ELLA. What? .

JIM. Nothing. (*After a pause – gropingly.*) I can't explain – just – but it hurts like fire. It brands me in my pride. I swear I know more'n any member of my class. I ought to, I study harder. I work like the devil. It's all in my head – all fine and correct to a T. Then when I'm called on – I stand up – all the white faces looking at me – and I can feel their eyes – I hear my own voice sounding funny, trembling – and all of a sudden it's all gone in my head – there's nothing remembered – and I hear myself stuttering – and give up – sit down – They don't laugh, hardly ever. They're kind. They're good people. (*In a frenzy.*) They're considerate, damn them! But I feel branded!

ELLA. Poor Jim!

JIM (*going on painfully*). And it's the same thing in the written exams. For weeks before I study all night. I can't sleep, anyway. I learn it all, I see it, I understand it. Then they give me the paper in the exam room. I look it over, I know each answer – perfectly. I take up my pen. On all sides are white men starting to write. They're so sure – even the ones that I know know nothing. But I know it all – but I can't remember any more – it fades – it goes – it's gone. There's a blank in my head – stupidity – I sit like a fool fighting to remember a little bit here, a little bit there – not enough to pass – not enough for anything – when I know it all!

ELLA (*compassionately*). Jim, it isn't worth it. You don't need to –

JIM. I need it more than anyone ever needed anything. I need it to live.

ELLA. What'll it prove?

JIM. Nothing at all much – but everything to me.

ELLA. You're so much better than they are in every other way.

JIM (*looking up at her*). Then – you understand?

ELLA. Of course. (*Affectionately.*) Don't I know how fine you've been to me! You've been the only one in the world who's stood by me – the only understanding person – and all after the rotten way I used to treat you.

JIM. But before that – way back so high – you treated me good. (*He smiles.*)

ELLA. You've been white to me, Jim. (*She takes his hand.*)

JIM. White – to you!

ELLA. Yes.

JIM. All love is white. I've always loved you. (*This with the deepest humility.*)

ELLA. Even now – after all that's happened!

JIM. Always.

ELLA. I like you, Jim – better than anyone else in the world.

JIM. That's more than enough, more than I ever hoped for. (*The organgrinder comes to the corner. He plays the chorus of 'Annie Laurie.' They sit listening, hand-in-hand.*) Would you ever want to marry me, Ella?

ELLA. Yes, Jim.

JIM (*as if this quick consent alarmed him*). No, no, don't answer now. Wait! Turn it over in your mind! Think what it means to you! Consider it – over and over again! I'm in no hurry, Ella. I can wait months – years –

ELLA. I'm alone. I've got to be helped. I've got to help someone – or it's the end – one end or another.

JIM (*eagerly*). Oh, I'll help you – I know I can help – I'll give my life to help you – that's what I've been living for –

ELLA. But can I help you? Can I help you?

JIM. Yes! Yes! We'll go abroad where a man is a man – where it don't make that difference – where people are kind and wise to see the soul under skins. I don't ask you to love me – I don't dare to hope nothing like that! I don't want nothing – only to wait – to know you like me – to be near you – to keep harm away – to make up for the past – to never let you suffer any more – to serve you – to lie at your feet like a dog that loves you – to kneel by your bed like a nurse that watches over you sleeping – to preserve and protect and shield you from evil and sorrow – to give my life and my blood and all the strength that's in me to give you peace and joy – to become your slave! – yes, be your slave – your black slave that adores you as sacred!

He has sunk to his knees. In a frenzy of self-abnegation, as he says the last words he beats his head on the flagstones.

ELLA (*overcome and alarmed*). Jim! Jim! You're crazy! I want to help you, Jim – I want to help –

Curtain.

Scene Four

Scene. – Some weeks or so later. A street in the same ward in front of an old brick church. The church stands back from the sidewalk in a yard enclosed by a rusty iron railing with a gate at centre. On each side of this yard are tenements. The buildings have a stern, forbidding look. All the shades on the windows are drawn down, giving an effect of staring, brutal eyes that pry callously at human beings without acknowledging them. Even the two tall, narrow church windows on either side of the arched door are blanked with dull green shades. It is a bright sunny morning. The district is unusually still, as if it were waiting, holding its breath.

From the street of the blacks to the right a Negro tenor sings in a voice of shadowy richness – the first stanza with a contented, childlike melancholy –

Sometimes I feel like a mourning dove,
Sometimes I feel like a mourning dove,
I feel like a mourning dove.

The second with a dreamy, boyish exultance –

Sometimes I feel like an eagle in the air,
Sometimes I feel like an eagle in the air,
I feel like an eagle in the air.

The third with a brooding, earthbound sorrow –

Sometimes I wish that I'd never been born,
Sometimes I wish that I'd never been born,
I wish that I'd never been born.

As the music dies down there is a pause of waiting stillness. This is broken by one startling, metallic clang of the church-bell. As if it were a signal, people – men, women, children – pour from the two tenements, whites from the tenement to the left, blacks from the one to the right. They hurry to form into two racial lines on each side of the gate, rigid and unyielding, staring across at each other with bitter hostile eyes. The halves of the big church door swing open and JIM *and* ELLA *step out from the darkness within into the sunlight. The doors slam behind them like wooden lips of an idol that has spat them out.* JIM *is dressed in black.* ELLA *in white, both with extreme plainness. They stand in the sunlight, shrinking and confused. All the hostile eyes are now concentrated on them. They become aware of the two lines through which they must pass; they hesitate and tremble; then stand there staring back at the people as fixed and immovable as they are. The organgrinder comes in from the right. He plays the chorus of 'Old Black Joe.' As he finishes the bell of the church clangs one more single stroke, insistently dismissing.*

JIM (*as if the sound had awakened him from a trance, reaches out and takes her hand*). Come. Time we got to the steamer. Time we sailed away over the sea. Come, Honey! (*She tries to answer, but her lips tremble; she cannot take her eyes off the eyes of the people; she is unable to move. He sees this and, keeping the same tone of profound, affectionate kindness, he points upward in the sky, and gradually persuades her eyes to look up.*) Look up, Honey! See the sun! Feel his warm eye lookin' down! Feel how kind he looks! Feel his blessing deep in your heart, your bones! Look up, Honey! (*Her eyes are fixed on the sky now. Her face is calm. She tries to smile bravely back at the sun. Now he pulls her by the hand, urging her gently to walk with him down through the yard and gate, through the lines of people. He is maintaining an attitude to support them through the ordeal only by a terrible effort, which manifests itself in the hysteric quality of ecstasy which breaks into his voice.*) And look at the sky! Ain't it kind and blue? Blue for hope. Don't they say blue's for hope? Hope! That's for us, Honey. All those blessings in the sky! What's it the Bible says? Falls on just and unjust alike? No, that's the sweet rain. Pshaw, what am I saying! All mixed up. There's no unjust about it. We're all the same – equally just – under the sky – under the sun – under God – sailing over the sea – to the other side of the world – the side where Christ was born – the kind side that takes count of the soul – over the sea – the sea's blue, to – Let's not be late – let's get that steamer! (*They have reached the kerb now, passed the lines of people. She is looking up to the sky with an expression of trance-like calm and peace. He is on the verge of collapse, his face twitching, his eyes staring. He calls hoarsely.*) Taxi! Where is he? Taxi!

Curtain.

ACT TWO

Scene One

Scene. Two years later. A flat of the better sort in the Negro district near the corner of Act One. This is the parlour. Its furniture is a queer clash. The old pieces are cheaply ornate, naïvely, childishly gaudy – the new pieces give evidence of a taste that is diametrically opposed, severe to the point of sombreness. On one wall, in a heavy gold frame, is a coloured photograph – the portrait of an elderly Negro with an able, shrewd face, but dressed in outlandish lodge regalia, a get-up adorned with medals, sashes, a cocked hat with frills – the whole effect as absurd to contemplate as one of Napoleon's Marshals in full uniform. In the left corner, where a window lights it effectively, is a Negro primitive mask from the Congo – a grotesque face, inspiring obscure, dim connotations in one's mind, but beautifully done, conceived in a true religious spirit. In this room, however, the mask acquires an arbitrary accentuation. It dominates by a diabolical quality that contrast imposes upon it.

There are two windows on the left looking out in the street. In the rear, a door to the hall of the building. In the right, a doorway with red and gold portières leading into the bedroom and the rest of the flat. Everything is cleaned and polished. The dark brown wallpaper is new, the brilliantly figured carpet also. There is a round mahogany table at centre. In a rocking-chair by the table MRS HARRIS *is sitting. She is a mild-looking, grey-haired Negress of sixty-five, dressed in an old-fashioned Sunday-best dress. Walking about the room nervously is* HATTIE, *her daughter,* JIM's *sister, a woman of about thirty with a high-strung, defiant face – an intelligent head showing both power and courage. She is dressed severely, mannishly.*

It is a fine morning in Spring. Sunshine comes through the windows at the left.

MRS HARRIS. Time dey was here, ain't it?

HATTIE (*impatiently*). Yes.

MRS HARRIS (*worriedly*). You ain't gwine ter kick up a fuss, is you – like you done wid Jim befo' de weddin'?

HATTIE. No. What's done is done.

MRS HARRIS. We mustn't let her see we hold it agin' her – de bad dat happened to her wid dat no–count fighter.

HATTIE. I certainly never give that a thought. It's what she's done to Jim – making him run away and give up his fight –!

MRS HARRIS. Jim loves her a powerful lot, must be.

HATTIE (*after a pause – bitterly*). I wonder if she loves Jim!

MRS HARRIS. She must, too. Yes, she must too. Don't you forget dat it was hard for her – mighty, mighty hard – harder for de white dan for de black!

HATTIE (*indignantly*). Why should it be?

MRS HARRIS (*shaking her head*). I ain't talkin' of shoulds. It's too late for shoulds. Dey's on'y one should. (*Solemnly.*) De white and de black shouldn't mix dat close. Dere's one road where de white goes on alone; dere's anudder road where de black goes on alone –

HATTIE. Yes, if they'd only leave us alone!

MRS HARRIS. Dey leaves your Pa alone. He comes to de top till he's got his own business, lots o' money in de bank, he owns a building even befo' he die. (*She looks up proudly at the picture. HATTIE sighs impatiently – then her mother goes on.*) Dey leaves me alone. I bears four children into dis worl', two dies, two lives. I helps you two grow up fine an' healthy and eddicated wid schoolin' and money fo' yo' comfort –

HATTIE (*impatiently*). Ma!

MRS HARRIS. I does de duty God set for me in dis' worl'. Dey leaves me alone. (*HATTIE goes to the window to hide her exasperation. The mother broods for a minute – then goes on.*) The worl' done change. Dey ain't no satisfaction wid nuffin' no more.

HATTIE. Oh! (*Then after a pause.*) They'll be here any minute now.

MRS HARRIS. Why didn't you go meet 'em at de dock like I axed you?

HATTIE. I couldn't. My face and Jim's among those hundreds of white faces – (*With a harsh laugh.*) It would give her too much advantage!

MRS HARRIS (*impatiently*). Don't talk dat way! What makes you so proud? (*Then after a pause – sadly.*) Hattie!

HATTIE (*turning*). Yes, Ma.

MRS HARRIS. I want to see Jim again – my only boy – but – all de same I'd ruther he stayed away. He say in his letter he's happy, she's happy, dey likes it dere, de folks don't think nuffin' but what's natural at seeing 'em married. Why don't dey stay?

HATTIE (*vehemently*). No! They were cowards to run away. If they believe in what they've done, then let them face it out, live it out here, be strong enough to conquer all prejudice!

MRS HARRIS. Strong? Dey ain't many strong. Dey ain't many happy neider. Dey was happy ovah yondah.

HATTIE. We don't deserve happiness till we've fought the fight of our race and won it! (*In the pause that follows there is a ring from back in the flat.*) It's the door bell! You go, Ma. I – I – I'd rather not. (*Her mother looks at her rebukingly and goes out agitatedly through the portières. HATTIE waits, nervously walking about, trying to compose herself. There is a long pause. Finally the portières are parted and* JIM *enters. He looks much older, graver, worried.*)

JIM. Hattie!

HATTIE. Jim! (*They embrace with great affection.*)

JIM. It's great to see you again! You're looking fine.

HATTIE (*looking at him searchingly*). You look well, too – thinner maybe – and tired. (*Then as she sees him frowning.*) But where's Ella?

JIM. With Ma. (*Apologetically.*) She sort of – broke down – when we came in. The trip wore her out.

HATTIE (*coldly*). I see.

JIM. Oh, it's nothing serious. Nerves. She needs a rest.

HATTIE. Wasn't living in France restful?

JIM. Yes, but – too lonely – especially for her.

HATTIE (*resentfully*). Why? Didn't the people there want to associate –

JIM (*quickly*). Oh, no indeed, they didn't think anything of that. (*After a pause.*) But – she did. For the first year it was all right. Ella liked everything a lot. She went out with French folks and got so she could talk it a little – and I learned it – a little. We were having a right nice time. I never thought then we'd ever want to come back here.

HATTIE (*frowning*). But – what happened to change you?

JIM (*after a pause – haltingly*). Well – you see – the first year – she and I were living around – like friends – like a brother and sister – like you and I might.

HATTIE (*her face becoming more and more drawn and tense*). You mean – then – ? (*She shudders – then after a pause.*) She loves you, Jim?

JIM. If I didn't know that I'd have to jump in the river.

HATTIE. Are you sure she loves you?

JIM. Isn't that why she's suffering?

HATTIE (*letting her breath escape through her clenched teeth*). Ah!

JIM (*suddenly springs up and shouts almost hysterically*). Why d'you ask me all those damn questions? Are you trying to make trouble between us?

HATTIE (*controlling herself – quietly*). No, Jim.

JIM (*after a pause – contritely*). I'm sorry, Hattie. I'm kind of on edge today. (*He sinks down on his chair – then goes on as if something forced him to speak.*) After that we got to living housed in. Ella didn't want to see nobody, she said just the two of us was enough. I was happy then – and I really guess she was happy, too – in a way – for a while. (*Again a pause.*) But she never did get to wanting to go out any place again. She got to saying she felt she'd be sure to run into someone she knew – from over here. So I moved us out to the country where no tourist ever comes – but it didn't make any difference to her. She got to avoiding the French folks the same as if they were Americans and I couldn't get it out of her mind. She lived in the house and got paler and paler, and more and more nervous and scarey, always imagining things – until I got to imagining things, too. I got to feeling blue. Got to sneering at myself that I wasn't any better than a quitter because I sneaked away right after getting married, didn't face nothing, gave up trying to become a Member of the Bar – and I got to suspecting Ella must feel that way about me, too – that I wasn't a *real man*!

HATTIE (*indignantly*). She couldn't!

JIM (*with hostility*). You don't need to tell me! All this was only in my own mind. We never quarrelled a single bit. We never said a harsh word. We were as close to each other as could be. We were all there was in the world to each other. We were alone together! (*A pause.*) Well, one day I got so I couldn't stand it. I could see she couldn't stand it. So I just up and said: Ella, we've got to have a plain talk, look everything straight in the face, hide nothing, come out with the exact truth of the way we feel.

HATTIE. And you decided to come back!

JIM. Yes. We decided the reason we felt sort of ashamed was we'd acted like cowards. We'd run away from the thing – and taken it with us. We decided to come back and face it and live it down in ourselves, and prove to ourselves we were strong in our love – and then, and that way only, by being brave we'd free ourselves, and gain confidence, and be really free inside and able then to go anywhere and live in peace and equality with ourselves and the world without any guilty uncomfortable feeling coming up to rile us. (*He has talked himself now into a state of happy confidence.*)

HATTIE (*bending over and kissing him*). Good for you! I admire you so much, Jim! I admire both of you! And you are going to begin studying right away and get admitted to the Bar?

JIM. You bet I am!

HATTIE. You must, Jim! Our race needs men like you to come to the front and help – (*As voices are heard approaching she stops, stiffens, and her face grows cold.*)

JIM (*noticing this – warningly*). Remember Ella's been sick! (*Losing control – threateningly.*) You be nice to her, you hear!

MRS HARRIS *enters, showing* ELLA *the way. The coloured woman is plainly worried and perplexed.* ELLA *is pale, with a strange, haunted expression in her eyes. She runs to* JIM *as to a refuge, clutching his hands in both of hers, looking from* MRS HARRIS *to* HATTIE *with a frightened defiance.*

MRS HARRIS. Dere he is, child, big's life! She was afraid we'd done kidnapped you away, Jim.

JIM (*patting her hand*). This place ought to be familiar, Ella. Don't you remember playing here with us sometimes as a kid?

ELLA (*queerly – with a frown of effort*). I remember playing marbles one night – but that was on the street.

JIM. Don't you remember Hattie?

HATTIE (*coming forward with a forced smile*). It was a long time ago – but I remember Ella. (*She holds out her hand.*)

ELLA (*taking it – looking at* HATTIE *with the same queer defiance*). I remember. But you've changed so much.

HATTIE (*stirred to hostility by* ELLA'*s manner – condescendingly*). Yes, I've grown older, naturally. (*Then in a tone which, as if in spite of herself, becomes bragging.*) I've worked so hard. First I went away to college, you know – then I took up post-graduate study – when suddenly I decided I'd accomplish more good if I gave up learning and took up teaching. (*She suddenly checks herself, ashamed, and stung by* ELLA'*s indifference.*) But this sounds like stupid boasting. I don't mean that. I was only explaining –

ELLA (*indifferently*). I didn't know you'd been to school so long. (*A pause.*) Where are you teaching? In a coloured school, I suppose. (*There is an indifferent superiority in her words that is maddening to* HATTIE.)

HATTIE (*controlling herself*). Yes. A private school endowed by some wealthy members of our race.

ELLA (*suddenly – even eagerly*). Then you must have taken lots of examinations and managed to pass them, didn't you?

HATTIE (*biting her lips*). I always passed with honours!

ELLA. Yes, we both graduated from the same High School, didn't we? That was dead easy for me. Why, I hardly even looked at a book. But Jim says it was awfully hard for him. He failed one year, remember?

She turns and smiles at JIM – *a tolerant, superior smile, but one full of genuine love.* HATTIE *is outraged, but* JIM *smiles.*

JIM. Yes, it was hard for me, Honey.

ELLA. And the law school examinations Jim hardly ever could pass at all. Could you? (*She laughs lovingly.*)

HATTIE (*harshly*). Yes, he could! He can! He'll pass them now – if you'll give him a chance!

JIM (*angrily*). Hattie!

MRS HARRIS. Hold yo' fool tongue!

HATTIE (*sullenly*). I'm sorry.

ELLA *has shrunk back against* JIM. *She regards* HATTIE *with a sort of wondering hatred. Then she looks away about the room.*

Suddenly her eyes fasten on the primitive mask and she gives a stifled scream.

JIM. What's the matter, Honey?

ELLA (*pointing*). That! For God's sake, what is it?

HATTIE (*scornfully*). It's a Congo mask. (*She goes and picks it up.*) I'll take it away if you wish. I thought you'd like it. It was my wedding present to Jim.

ELLA. What is it?

HATTIE. It's a mask which used to be worn in religious ceremonies by my people in Africa. But, aside from that, it's beautifully made, a work of Art by a real artist – as real in his way as your Michael Angelo. (*Forces* ELLA *to take it.*) Here. Just notice the workmanship.

ELLA (*defiantly*). I'm not scared of it if you're not. (*Looking at it with disgust.*) Beautiful? Well, some people certainly have queer notions! It looks ugly to me and stupid – like a kid's game – making faces! (*She slaps it contemptuously.*) Pooh! You needn't look hard at me. I'll give you the laugh. (*She goes to put it back on the stand.*)

JIM. Maybe, if it disturbs you, we better put it in some other room.

ELLA (*defiantly aggressive*). No. I want it here where I can give it the laugh! (*She sets it there again – then turns suddenly on* HATTIE *with aggressive determination.*) Jim's not going to take any more examinations! I won't let him!

HATTIE (*bursting forth*). Jim! Do you hear that? There's white justice! – their fear for their superiority –

ELLA (*with a terrified pleading*). Make her go away. Jim!

JIM (*losing control – furiously to his sister*). Either you leave here – or we will!

MRS HARRIS (*weeping – throws her arms around* HATTIE). Let's go, chile! Let's go!

HATTIE (*calmly now*). Yes, Ma. All right.

They go through the portières. As soon as they are gone, JIM *suddenly collapses into a chair and hides his head in his hands.* ELLA *stands beside him for a moment. She stares distractedly about her, at the portrait, at the mask, at the furniture, at* JIM. *She seems fighting to escape from some weight on her mind. She throws this off and completely her old self for the moment, kneels by* JIM *and pats his shoulder.*

ELLA (*with kindness and love*). Don't, Jim! Don't cry, please! You don't suppose I really meant that about the examinations, do you? Why, of course, I didn't mean a word! I couldn't mean it! I want you to take the examinations! I want you to pass! I want you to be a lawyer! I want you to be the best lawyer in the country! I want you to show 'em – all the dirty sneaking, gossiping liars that talk behind our backs – what a man I married. I want the whole world to know you're the whitest of the white! I want you to climb and climb – and step on 'em, stamp right on their mean faces! I love you, Jim. You know that!

JIM (*calm again – happily*). I hope so, Honey – and I'll make myself worthy.

HATTIE (*appears in the doorway – quietly*). We're going now, Jim.

ELLA. No. Don't go.

HATTIE. We were going to, anyway. This is your house – Mother's gift to you, Jim.

JIM (*astonished*). But I can't accept – Where are you going?

HATTIE. We've got a nice flat in the Bronx – (*With bitter pride.*) in the heart of the Black Belt – the Congo – among our own people!

JIM (*angrily*). You're crazy – I'll see Ma –

He goes out. HATTIE *and* ELLA *stare at each other with scorn and hatred for a moment, then* HATTIE *goes.* ELLA *remains kneeling for a moment by the chair, her eyes dazed and strange as she looks about her. Then she gets to her feet and stands before the portrait of* JIM's *father – with a sneer.*

ELLA. It's his Old Man – all dolled up like a circus horse! Well, they can't help it. It's in the blood, I suppose. They're ignorant, that's all there is to it. (*She moves to the mask – forcing a mocking tone.*) Hello, sport! Who d'you think you're scaring? Not me! I'll give you the laugh. He won't pass, you wait and see. Not in a thousand years! (*She goes to the window and looks down at the street and mutters.*) All black! Every one of them! (*Then with sudden excitement.*) No, there's one. Why, it's Shorty! (*She throws the window open and calls.*) Shorty! Shorty! Hello, Shorty! (*She leans out and waves – then stops, remains there for a moment looking down, then comes back into the room suddenly as if she wanted to hide – her whole face in an anguish.*) Say! Say! I wonder? – No, he didn't hear you. Yes, he did too! He must have! I yelled so loud you could hear me in Jersey! No, what are you talking about? How would he hear me with all kids yelling down there? He never heard a word, I tell you! He did, too! He didn't want to hear you! He didn't want to let anyone know he knew you! Why don't you acknowledge it? What are you lying about? I'm not! Why shouldn't he! Where does he come in to – for God's sake, who is Shorty, anyway? A pimp! Yes, and a dope-pedlar, too! D'you mean to say he'd have the nerve to hear me call him and then deliberately – ? Yes, I mean to say it! I do say it! And it's true, and you know it, and you might as well be honest for a change and admit it! He heard you, but he didn't want to hear you! He doesn't want to know you any more. No, not even him! He's afraid it'd get him in wrong with the old gang. Why? You know well enough! Because you married a – a – a – well, I won't say it, but you know without my mentioning names! (ELLA *springs to her feet in horror and shakes off her obsession like a frightened child.*) Jim! Jim! Jim! Where are you? I want you, Jim!

She runs out of the room as the curtain falls.

Scene Two

Scene. The same. Six months later. It is evening. The walls of the room appear shrunken in, the ceiling lowered, so that the furniture, the portrait, the mask, look unnaturally large and domineering. JIM *is seated at the table studying, law books piled by his elbows. He is keeping his attention concentrated only by a driving physical effort which gives his face the expression of a runner's near the tape. His forehead shines with perspiration. He mutters one sentence from Blackstone over and over again, tapping his forehead with his fist in time to the rhythm he gives the stale words. But, in spite of himself, his attention wanders, his eyes have an uneasy, hunted look, he starts at every sound in the house or from the street. Finally, he remains rigid, Blackstone forgotten, his eyes fixed on the portières with tense grief. Then he groans, slams the book shut, goes to the window and throws it open and sinks down beside it, his arms on the sill, his head resting wearily on his arms, staring out into the night, the pale glare from the arc-lamp on the corner throwing his face into relief. The portières on the right are parted and* HATTIE *comes in.*

HATTIE (*not seeing him at the table*). Jim! (*Discovering him.*) Oh, there you are! What're you doing?

JIM (*turning to her*). Resting. Cooling my head. (*Forcing a smile.*) These law books certainly are a sweating proposition! (*Then, anxiously.*) How is she?

HATTIE. She's asleep now. I felt it was safe to leave her for a minute. (*After a pause.*) What did the doctor tell you, Jim?

JIM. The same old thing. She must have rest, he says, her mind needs rest – (*Bitterly.*) But he can't tell me any prescription for that rest – leastways not any that'd work.

HATTIE (*after a pause*). I think you ought to leave her, Jim – or let her leave you – for a while, anyway.

JIM (*angrily*). You're like the doctor. Everything's so simple and easy. Do this and that happens. Only it don't. Life isn't simple like that – not in this case, anyway – no, it isn't simple a bit. (*After a pause.*) I can't leave her. She can't leave me. And there's a million little reasons combining to make one big reason why we can't. (*A pause.*) For her sake – if it'd do her good – I'd go – I'd leave – I'd do anything – because I love her. I'd kill myself even – jump out of this window this second – I've thought it over, too – but that'd only make matters worse for her. I'm all she's got in the world! Yes, that isn't bragging or fooling myself. I know that for a fact! Don't you know that's true? (*There is a pleading for the certainty he claims.*)

HATTIE. Yes, I know she loves you, Jim. I know that now.

JIM (*simply*). Then we've got to stick together to the end, haven't we, whatever comes – and hope and pray for the best? (*A pause – then hopefully.*) I think maybe this is the crisis in her mind. Once she settles this in herself, she's won to the other side. And me – once I become a Member of the Bar – then I win, too! We're both free – by our own fighting down our own weakness! We're both really, truly free! Then we can be happy with ourselves here or anywhere. She'll be proud then! Yes, she's told me again and again, she says she'll be actually proud!

HATTIE (*turning away to conceal her emotion*). Yes, I'm sure – but you mustn't study too hard, Jim! You mustn't study too awfully hard!

JIM (*gets up and goes to the table and sits down wearily*). Yes, I know. Oh, I'll pass easily. I haven't got any scarey feeling about that any more. And I'm doing two years' work in one here alone. That's better than schools, eh?

HATTIE (*doubtfully*). It's wonderful, Jim.

JIM (*his spirit evaporating*). If I can only hold out! It's hard! I'm worn out. I don't sleep. I get to thinking and thinking. My head aches and burns like fire with thinking. Round and round my thoughts go chasing like crazy chickens hopping and flapping before the wind. It gets me crazy mad – 'cause I can't stop!

HATTIE (*watching him for a while and seeming to force herself to speak*). The doctor didn't tell you all, Jim.

JIM (*dully*). What's that?

HATTIE. He told me you're liable to break down too, if you don't take care of yourself.

JIM (*abjectly weary*). Let 'er come! I don't care what happens to me. Maybe if I get sick she'll get well. There's only so much bad luck allowed to one family, maybe. (*He forces a wan smile.*)

HATTIE (*hastily*). Don't give in to that idea, for the Lord's sake!

JIM. I'm tired – and blue – that's all.

HATTIE (*after another long pause*). I've got to tell you something else, Jim.

JIM (*dully*). What?

HATTIE. The doctor said Ella's liable to be sick like this a very long time.

JIM. He told me that, too – that it'd be a long time before she got back her normal strength. Well, I suppose that's got to be expected.

HATTIE (*slowly*). He didn't mean convalescing – what he told me. (*A long pause.*)

JIM (*evasively*). I'm going to get other doctors in to see Ella – specialists. This one's a damn fool.

HATTIE. Be sensible, Jim. You'll have to face the truth – sooner or later.

JIM (*irritably*). I know the truth about Ella better'n any doctor.

HATTIE (*persuasively*). She'd get better so much sooner if you'd send her away to some nice sanatorium –

JIM. No! She'd die of shame there!

HATTIE. At least until after you've taken your examinations –

JIM. To hell with me!

HATTIE. Six months. That wouldn't be long to be parted.

JIM. What are you trying to do – separate us? (*He gets to his feet – furiously.*) Go on out! Go on out!

HATTIE (*calmly*). No, I won't. (*Sharply.*) There's something that's got to be said to you and I'm the only one with the courage – (*Intensely.*) Tell me, Jim, have you heard her raving when she's out of her mind?

JIM (*with a shudder*). No!

HATTIE. You're lying, Jim. You must have – if you don't stop your ears – and the doctor says she may develop a violent mania, dangerous for you – get worse and worse until – Jim, you'll go crazy, too – living this way. Today she raved on about 'Black! Black!' and cried because she said her skin was turning black – that you had poisoned her –

JIM (*in anguish*). That's only when she's out of her mind.

HATTIE. And then she suddenly called me a dirty nigger.

JIM. No! She never said that ever! She never would!

HATTIE. She did – and kept on and on! (*A tense pause.*) She'll be saying that to you soon.

JIM (*torturedly*). She don't mean it! She isn't responsible for what she's saying!

HATTIE. I know she isn't – yet she is just the same. It's deep down in her or it wouldn't come out.

JIM. Deep down in her people – not deep in her.

HATTIE. I can't make such distinctions. The race in me, deep in me, can't stand it. I can't play nurse to her any more, Jim, – not even for your sake. I'm afraid – afraid of myself – afraid sometime I'll kill her dead to set you free! (*She loses control and begins to cry.*)

JIM (*after a long pause – sombrely*). Yes, I guess you'd better stay away from here. Goodbye.

HATTIE. Who'll you get to nurse her, Jim, – a white woman?

JIM. Ella'd die of shame. No, I'll nurse her myself.

HATTIE. And give up your studies?

JIM. I can do both.

HATTIE. You can't! You'll get sick yourself! Why, you look terrible even as it is – and it's only beginning!

JIM. I can do anything for her! I'm all she's got in the world! I've got to prove I can be all to her! I've got to prove worthy! I've got to prove she can be proud of me! I've got to prove I'm the whitest of the white!

HATTIE (*stung by this last – with rebellious bitterness*). Is that the ambition she's given you? Oh, you soft, weak-minded fool, you traitor to your race! And the thanks you'll get – to be called a dirty nigger – to hear her cursing you because she can never have a child because it'll be born black –

JIM (*in a frenzy*). Stop!

HATTIE. I'll say what must be said even though you kill me, Jim. Send her to an asylum before you both have to be sent to one together.

JIM (*with a sudden wild laugh*). Do you think you're threatening me with something dreadful now? Why, I'd like that. Sure, I'd like that! Maybe she'd like it better, too. Maybe we'd both find it all simple then – like you think it is now. Yes. (*He laughs again.*)

HATTIE (*frightenedly*). Jim!

JIM. Together! You can't scare me even with hell fire if you say she and I go together. It's heaven then for me! (*With sudden savagery.*) You go out of here! All you've ever been aiming to do is to separate us so we can't be together!

HATTIE. I've done what I did for your own good.

JIM. I have no own good. I only got a good together with her. I'm all she's got in the world! Let her call me nigger! Let her call me the whitest of the white! I'm all she's got in the world, ain't I? She's all I've got! You with your fool talk of the black race and the white race! Where does the human race get a chance to come in? I suppose that's simple for you. You lock it up in asylums and throw away the key! (*With fresh violence.*) Go along! There isn't going to be no more people coming in here to separate – excepting the doctor. I'm going to lock the door, and it's going to stay locked, you hear? Go along, now!

HATTIE (*confusedly*). Jim!

JIM (*pushes her out gently and slams the door after her – vaguely*). Go along! I got to study. I got to nurse Ella, too. Oh, I can do it! I can do anything for her!

He sits down at the table and, opening the book, begins again to recite the lines from Blackstone in a meaningless rhythm, tapping his

forehead with his fist. ELLA *enters noiselessly through the portières.
She wears a red dressing-gown over her night-dress but is in her bare
feet. She has a carving-knife in her right hand. Her eyes fasten on*
JIM *with a murderous mania. She creeps up behind him. Suddenly he
senses something and turns. As he sees her he gives a cry, jumping up
and catching her wrist. She stands fixed, her eyes growing bewildered
and frightened.*

JIM (*aghast*). Ella! For God's sake! Do you want to murder me?
(*She does not answer. He shakes her.*)

ELLA (*whisperingly*). They kept calling me names as I was walking
along – I can't tell you what, Jim – and then I grabbed a knife –

JIM. Yes! See! This! (*She looks at it frightenedly.*)

ELLA. Where did I – ? I was having a nightmare – Where did
they go – I mean, how did I get here? (*With sudden terrified
pleading – like a little girl.*) Oh, Jim – don't ever leave me alone!
I have such terrible dreams, Jim – promise you'll never go
away!

JIM. I promise, Honey.

ELLA (*her manner becoming more and more childishly silly*). I'll be a
little girl – and you'll be old Uncle Jim who's been with us for
years and years – Will you play that?

JIM. Yes, Honey. Now you better go back to bed.

ELLA (*like a child*). Yes, Uncle Jim. (*She turns to go. He pretends to
be occupied by his book. She looks at him for a second – then suddenly
asks in her natural woman's voice.*) Are you studying hard, Jim?

JIM. Yes, Honey. Go to bed now. You need to rest, you know.

ELLA (*stands looking at him, fighting with herself. A startling
transformation comes over her face. It grows mean, vicious, full of
jealous hatred. She cannot contain herself, but breaks out harshly with
a cruel, venomous grin.*) You dirty nigger!

JIM (*starting as if he'd been shot.*) Ella! For the good Lord's sake!

ELLA (*coming out of her insane mood for a moment, aware of something
terrible, frightened*). Jim! Jim! Why are you looking at me like
that?

JIM. What did you say to me just then!

ELLA (*gropingly*). Why, I – I said – I remember saying, are you
studying hard, Jim? Why? You're not mad at that, are you?

JIM. No, Honey. What made you think I was mad? Go to bed now.

ELLA (*obediently*). Yes, Jim. (*She passes behind the portières. JIM stares before him. Suddenly her head is thrust out at the side of the portières. Her face is again that of a vindictive maniac.*) Nigger! (*The face disappears – she can be heard running away, laughing with cruel satisfaction. JIM bows his head on his outstretched arms, but he is too stricken for tears.*)

Curtain.

Scene Three

Scene. The same, six months later. The sun has just gone down. The Spring twilight sheds a vague, grey light about the room, picking out the Congo mask on the stand by the window. The walls have shrunken in still more, the ceiling now barely clears the people's heads, the furniture and the characters appear enormously magnified. Law books are stacked in two great piles on each side of the table. ELLA comes in from the right, the carving-knife in her hand. She is pitifully thin, her face is wasted, but her eyes glow with a mad energy, her movements are abrupt and spring-like. She looks stealthily about the room, then advances and stands before the mask, her arms akimbo, her attitude one of crazy mockery, fear and bravado. She is dressed in the red dressing-gown, grown dirty and ragged now, and is in her bare feet.

ELLA. I'll give you the laugh, wait and see! (*Then in a confidential tone.*) He thought I was asleep! He called, Ella, Ella – but I kept my eyes shut, I pretended to snore. I fooled him good. (*She gives a little hoarse laugh.*) This is the first time he's dared to leave me alone for months and months. I've been wanting to talk to you every day, but this is the only chance – (*With sudden violence – flourishing her knife.*) What're you grinning about, you dirty nigger, you? How dare you grin at me? I guess you forget what you are! That's always the way. Be kind to you, treat you decent, and in a second you've got a swelled head, you think you're somebody, you're all over the place putting on airs. Why, it's got so I can't even walk down the street without seeing niggers, niggers everywhere. Hanging around, grinning, grinning – going to school – pretending they're white – taking examinations – (*She stops, arrested by the word, then suddenly.*) That's where he's gone – down to the mail-box – to see if there's a letter from the Board – telling him – But why is he so long? (*She calls pitifully.*) Jim! (*Then in a terrified whimper.*) Maybe he's passed! Maybe he's passed! (*In a frenzy.*) No! No! He can't! I'd kill him! I'd kill myself! (*Threatening the Congo mask.*) It's you who're to blame for this! Yes, you! Oh, I'm on to you! (*Then appealingly.*) But why d'you want to do this to us? What have I ever done wrong to you? What have you got against me? I married you, didn't I? Why don't you let Jim alone? Why don't you let him be happy as he is – with me? Why don't you let me be happy? He's white, isn't he – the whitest man that ever lived? Where do you come in to interfere? Black! Black! Black as dirt! You've poisoned me! I can't wash myself clean! Oh, I hate you! I hate you! Why don't you let Jim and I be happy?

She sinks down in his chair, her arms outstretched on the table. The door from the hall is slowly opened and JIM *appears. His bloodshot, sleepless eyes stare from deep hollows. His expression is one of crushed, numbness. He holds an open letter in his hand.*

JIM (*seeing* ELLA – *in an absolutely dead voice*). Honey – I thought you were asleep.

ELLA (*starts and wheels about in her chair*). What's that? You got – you got a letter – ?

JIM (*turning to close the door after him*). From the Board of Examiners for admission to the Bar, State of New York – God's country! (*He finishes up with a chuckle of ironic self-pity so spent as to be barely audible.*)

ELLA (*writhing out of her chair like some fierce animal, the knife held behind her – with fear and hatred*). You didn't – you didn't – you didn't pass, did you?

JIM (*looking at her wildly*). Pass? Pass? (*He begins to chuckle and laugh between sentences and phrases, rich, Negro laughter, but heart-breaking in its mocking grief.*) Good Lord, child, how come you can ever imagine such a crazy idea? Pass? Me? Jim Crow Harris? Nigger Jim Harris – become a full-fledged Member of the Bar! Why, the mere notion of it is enough to kill you with laughing! It'd be against all natural laws, all human rights and justice. It'd be miraculous, there'd be earthquakes and catastrophes, the Seven Plagues'd come again and locusts'd devour all the money in the banks, the second Flood'd come roaring and Noah'd fall overboard, the sun'd drop out of the sky like a ripe fig, and the Devil'd perform miracles, and God'd be tipped head first right out of the Judgment Seat! (*He laughs, maudlinly uproarious.*)

ELLA (*her face beginning to relax, to light up*). Then you – you
didn't pass?

JIM (*spent – giggling and gasping idiotically*). Well, I should say not!
I should certainly say not!

ELLA (*with a cry of joy, pushes all the law books crashing to the floor –
then with childish happiness she grabs* JIM *by both hands and dances
up and down.*) Oh, Jim, I knew it! I knew you couldn't! Oh, I'm
so glad, Jim! I'm so happy! You're still my old Jim – and I'm so
glad! (*He looks at her dazedly, a fierce rage slowly gathering on his
face. She dances away from him. His eyes follow her. His hands clench.
She stands in front of the mask – triumphantly.*) There! What did I
tell you? I told you I'd give you the laugh! (*She begins to laugh
with wild unrestraint, grabs the mask from its place, sets it in the
middle of the table and plunging the knife down through it pins it to
the table.*) There! Who's got the laugh now?

JIM (*his eyes bulging – hoarsely*). You devil! You white devil
woman! (*In a terrible roar, raising his fists above her head.*) You
devil!

ELLA (*looking up at him with a bewildered cry of terror*). Jim! (*Her
appeal recalls him to himself. He lets his arms slowly drop to his sides,
bowing his head.* ELLA *points tremblingly to the mask.*) It's all right,
Jim! It's dead. The devil's dead. See! It couldn't live – unless
you passed. If you'd passed it would have lived in you. Then
I'd have had to kill you, Jim, don't you see – or it would have
killed me. But now I've killed it. (*She pats his hand.*) So you
needn't ever be afraid any more, Jim.

JIM (*dully*). I've got to sit down, Honey. I'm tired. I haven't had
much chance for sleep in so long – (*He slumps down in the chair
by the table.*)

ELLA (*sits down on the floor beside him and holds his hand. Her face is
gradually regaining an expression that is happy, childlike, and pretty*).
I know, Jim! That was my fault. I wouldn't let you sleep. I
couldn't let you. I kept thinking if he sleeps good then he'll be
sure to study good and then he'll pass – and the devil'll win!

JIM (*with a groan*). Don't, Honey!

ELLA (*with a childish grin*). That was why I carried that knife
around – (*she frowns – puzzled*) – one reason – to keep you from
studying and sleeping by scaring you.

JIM. I wasn't scared of being killed. I was scared of what they'd
do to you after.

ELLA (*after a pause – like a child*). Will God forgive me, Jim?

JIM. Maybe He can forgive what you've done to me; and maybe He can forgive what I've done to you; but I don't see how He's going to forgive – Himself.

ELLA. I prayed and prayed. When you were away taking the examinations and I was alone with the nurse, I closed my eyes and pretended to be asleep, but I was praying with all my might: O God, don't let Jim pass!

JIM (*with a sob*). Don't, Honey, don't! For the good Lord's sake! You're hurting me!

ELLA (*frightenedly*). How, Jim? Where? (*Then after a pause – suddenly.*) I'm sick, Jim. I don't think I'll live long.

JIM (*simply*). Then I won't either. Somewhere yonder maybe – together – our luck'll change. But I wanted – here and now – before you – we – I wanted to prove to you – to myself – to become a full-fledged Member – so you could be proud – (*He stops. Words fail and he is beyond tears.*)

ELLA (*brightly*). Well, it's all over, Jim. Everything'll be all right now. (*Chattering along.*) I'll be just your little girl, Jim – and you'll be my little boy – just as we used to be, remember, when we were beaux; and I'll put shoe blacking on my face and pretend I'm black, and you can put chalk on your face and pretend you're white, just as we used to do – and we can play marbles – only you mustn't all the time be a boy. Sometimes you must be my old kind Uncle Jim who's been with us for years and years. Will you, Jim?

JIM (*with utter resignation*). Yes, Honey.

ELLA. And you'll never, never, never, never leave me, Jim?

JIM. Never, Honey.

ELLA. 'Cause you're all I've got in the world – and I love you, Jim. (*She kisses his hand as a child might, tenderly and gratefully.*)

JIM (*suddenly throws himself on his knees and raises his shining eyes, his transfigured face*). Forgive me, God – and make me worthy! Now I see Your Light again! Now I hear Your Voice! (*He begins to weep in an ectasy of religious humility.*) Forgive me, God, for blaspheming You! Let this fire of burning suffering purify me of selfishness and make me worthy of the child You send me for the woman You take away!

ELLA (*jumping to her feet – excitedly*). Don't cry, Jim! You mustn't cry! I've got only a little time left and I want to play. Don't be old Uncle Jim now. Be my little boy, Jim. Pretend you're Painty Face and I'm Jim Crow. Come and play!

JIM (*still deeply exalted*). Honey. Honey, I'll play right up to the gates of heaven with you!

She tugs at one of his hands, laughingly trying to pull him up from his knees as the curtain falls.